Vegetables

GENERAL EDITOR
CHUCK WILLIAMS

RECIPES
EMALEE CHAPMAN

PHOTOGRAPHY
ALLAN ROSENBERG

TIME
LIFE
BOOKS

Time-Life Books
is a division of TIME LIFE INC.,
a wholly owned subsidiary of
THE TIME INC. BOOK COMPANY

President: John M. Fahey

TIME-LIFE BOOKS
President: John Hall
Vice President and Publisher, Custom Publishing:
    Susan J. Maruyama
Director of Custom Publishing: Frances C. Mangan
Director of Marketing: Nancy K. Jones

WILLIAMS-SONOMA
Founder/Vice-Chairman: Chuck Williams

WELDON OWEN INC.
President: John Owen
Publisher: Wendely Harvey
Managing Editor: Laurie Wertz
Consulting Editor: Norman Kolpas
Copy Editor: Sharon Silva
Editorial Assistant: Janique Poncelet
Design: John Bull, The Book Design Company
Production: Stephanie Sherman, Mick Bagnato
Food Photographer: Allan Rosenberg
Associate Food Photographer: Allen V. Lott
Primary Food & Prop Stylist: Sandra Griswold
Food Stylist: Heidi Gintner
Assistant Food Stylist: Danielle Di Salvo
Prop Assistant: Karen Nicks
Glossary Illustrations: Alice Harth

The Williams-Sonoma Kitchen Library
conceived and produced by Weldon Owen Inc.
814 Montgomery St., San Francisco, CA 94133

In collaboration with Williams-Sonoma
100 North Point, San Francisco, CA 94133

Production by Mandarin Offset, Hong Kong
Printed in China

A Note on Weights and Measures:
All recipes include customary U.S., U.K. and
metric measurements. Conversions are based on
a standard developed for these books and have
been rounded off. Actual weights may vary.

A Weldon Owen Production

Copyright © 1993 Weldon Owen Inc.
All rights reserved, including the right of
reproduction in whole or in part in any form.

Library of Congress
Cataloging-in-Publication Data:

Chapman, Emalee.
    Vegetables / general editor, Chuck Williams ;
recipes, Emalee Chapman ; photography,
Allan Rosenberg.
        p.   cm. — (Williams-Sonoma
    kitchen library)
    Includes index.
    ISBN 0-7835-0254-0 (trade) ;
    ISBN 0-7835-0255-9 (library)
    1. Cookery (Vegetables)   I. Williams, Chuck.
II. Title.   III. Series.
TX801.C43   1993
641.6'5—dc20   93-17991
                                            CIP

Contents

VEGETABLES FOR ALL SEASONS 17

SPRING & SUMMER VEGETABLES 33

FALL & WINTER VEGETABLES 75

INTRODUCTION

"Eat your vegetables!" How many people, I wonder, still dread those words, no matter how far away their childhood years may be?

Vegetables have long suffered under the misguided belief that something that is good for you can't possibly taste good. Yet, our ever-widening knowledge about nutrition points to the undeniable fact that everyone should include more vegetables in their meals.

This book is dedicated to the goal of making vegetables as attractive to serve and delicious to eat as they are healthful and nutritious. It begins with a brief survey of the basics of vegetable cookery: kitchen equipment, selecting and storing vegetables, peeling and cutting techniques, cooking methods and basic sauces. These fundamentals are followed by 44 recipes, organized by their main ingredients' seasonal availability.

I'm a firm believer in letting the seasons dictate which vegetables to eat. Modern air-freight systems make it possible to get just about any vegetable we want at any time of the year. But the vegetables that taste best will always be those that grow when nature intends them to grow, are picked at their peak of ripeness and are cooked as soon after that as possible. To help you purchase and cook vegetables at their optimum, seek out one of the good small fruit and vegetable shops that are springing up everywhere, or one of the farmers' markets that allow growers from the country to bring their finest products to the heart of the city.

Buy the finest-quality ingredients and cook them in one of the many simple ways shown on these pages, and I'm sure you'll begin to see vegetables in a whole new light. And rather than serving them only as side dishes, try making some of the recipes the stars of your dinner table.

Please join me in transforming the phrase "Eat your vegetables!" into a happy rallying cry.

EQUIPMENT

Basic cookware and utensils match the utter simplicity of vegetables themselves

The simple range of equipment shown here reflects how easy it is to prepare and cook vegetables. Pots and pans of various capacities, for example, efficiently boil, steam, sauté, fry or braise vegetables of any size or shape. Ovenproof porcelain dishes hold baked whole vegetables, gratins and puddings.

A few tools help yield excellent results. Good-quality sharp knives and a vegetable peeler will streamline ingredient preparation. And a sturdy, old-fashioned ricer will purée boiled vegetables in less time than it takes to assemble a food processor.

1. Sauté Pan
For sautéing or boiling. Select a well-made heavy metal pan large enough to hold ingredients without crowding. Straight sides, usually about 2½ inches (6 cm) high, help contain splattering and permit boiling of small pieces or quantities of vegetables. Close-fitting lid covers pan for slower, gentler cooking.

2. Frying Pan
Choose good-quality, heavy aluminum, stainless steel, cast iron or enamel for rapid browning or frying, or for boiling small quantities or pieces of vegetables. Sloped, shallow sides facilitate stirring or turning of vegetable pieces and allow moisture to escape more easily for better browning.

3. Stockpot
Tall, deep, large-capacity pot with close-fitting lid, for making stock or for boiling or steaming large quantities of vegetables. Select a good-quality heavy pot that absorbs and transfers heat well. Enamelware, shown here, cleans easily and does not react with the acidity of any wine, citrus juice or tomatoes added during cooking.

4. Gratin Dish
Traditional shallow French-style dish for baked vegetables, particularly those in which a well-browned crust (gratin) is desired. Choose heavy-duty glazed porcelain, stoneware, earthenware or ovenproof glass. Available in a variety of shapes and sizes.

5. Wooden Spoon
Wide bowl and sturdy handle allow efficient stirring of vegetable casseroles, purées and sauces.

6. Metal Spoon
For stirring sauces, casseroles and purées, and for basting baked vegetable dishes.

7. Slotted Spoon
For stirring sauces, casseroles and purées, and for removing and draining pieces of vegetable from liquids in which they have cooked.

8. Soufflé Dish
For baking and serving vegetables, usually puddings. Choose good-quality glazed porcelain, earthenware or ovenproof glass.

9. Ricer
For puréeing boiled or steamed vegetables, which are put in the basket of its lower half and forced through small holes when the hinged upper handle is closed. Choose a sturdy stainless-steel model. Particularly useful for puréeing potatoes, which acquire a gummy texture if puréed in a food processor.

10. Wire Whisk
For whisking sauces, particularly béchamel or other milk-based sauces.

11. Colander
For straining solids from stock and for draining boiled vegetables.

12. Sieve
For sieving sauces, straining stock and draining boiled vegetables.

13. Saucepans
For boiling or braising vegetables, or for simmering sauces.

14. Wok
Heavy-duty steel or aluminum spherical pan for rapid stir-frying or sautéing of small pieces of vegetable.

15. Ring Mold
Circular mold with a center hole, for baking relatively moist vegetable mixtures. Unmolds for an attractive ring-shaped presentation.

16. Dish Towel
Good-quality cotton towel for general kitchen cleanup.

17. Pot Holder
Heavy-duty cotton provides good protection from hot cookware.

18. Baking Dish
For baked vegetables, particularly those to be served directly from the dish. Choose heavy, heatproof porcelain, glazed earthenware or glass.

19. Vegetable Peeler
Curved, slotted swiveling blade thinly strips away vegetable peels. Choose a sturdy model that feels comfortable in your hand.

20. Chef's Knife and Paring Knife
Larger all-purpose chef's knife for chopping and slicing large items or large quantities of ingredients. Smaller paring knife for peeling and paring vegetables and cutting up small ingredients. Choose sturdy knives with sharp stainless-steel blades securely attached to sturdy handles that feel comfortable in the hand.

CHOOSING AND STORING YOUR VEGETABLES

Simple guidelines for selecting the best-quality ingredients and maintaining them in optimum condition

For the highest quality, buy vegetables from a market with good suppliers and a regular turnover. Small specialty stands and local farmers' markets may offer a better and wider selection. Locally grown vegetables in season will invariably taste best and cost less than their greenhouse-grown or air-freighted competition. Or better yet, grow your own.

Fresh vegetables actually *look* fresh. Avoid any that are limp, discolored, shriveled, cracked or otherwise past their peak. Cook them as soon as possible after purchase or harvesting. If you need to store them, follow the guidelines below. When refrigerating vegetables, always store them in your refrigerator's vegetable compartment.

Artichokes. Refrigerate in an open plastic bag for up to 3 days.

Cabbage family. Refrigerate cabbages, Brussels sprouts, kohlrabi, cauliflower, bok choy and broccoli in an open paper bag for up to 3 days.

Corn. Refrigerate unhusked in an open plastic bag for up to 2 days. Corn is one vegetable that definitely tastes better if cooked within 1 or 2 hours of picking.

Leaf vegetables. Refrigerate in open plastic bags for up to 3 days.

Mushrooms. Refrigerate in an open paper bag for up to 3 days.

Onions. Keep dry-skinned onions loose in a cool, dark, dry place for up to several weeks. Refrigerate green (spring) onions and leeks for up to 1 week.

Peas and beans. Refrigerate fresh peas and beans in an open plastic bag for up to 3 days.

Root vegetables. Store all kinds of mature potatoes, as well as rutabagas (swedes), for up to several weeks in open paper bags in a cool, dark, dry, airy place. Refrigerate new potatoes and Jerusalem artichokes in open plastic bags for up to 3 days; beets (beetroots), celeriac (celery root) and parsnips for up to 1 week; and carrots and turnips for up to 2 weeks.

Stalks. Refrigerate asparagus in an open plastic bag for up to 2 days, and celery and fennel bulbs in an open plastic bag for up to 5 days.

Fruit vegetables and squashes. Eat ripe tomatoes immediately; store underripe tomatoes at cool room temperature. Refrigerate cucumbers, zucchini (courgettes), peppers (capsicums) and eggplants (aubergines), unwrapped for up to several days, and okra in an open plastic bag for the same amount of time. Store hard-shelled squashes at room temperature for up to several weeks.

PREPARING VEGETABLES FOR COOKING

Trimming, peeling, paring, slicing, dicing and chopping all manner of vegetables

Both practical and aesthetic considerations are involved in the way you prepare vegetables for cooking. Most vegetables are at the very least trimmed of their coarse or unattractive stem ends. Many are also peeled to remove their tough, rough-textured or discolored skins.

The way a vegetable is cut up clearly has an effect upon a recipe's final appearance. Neat, uniform dice or diagonal slices, for example, can be far more pleasing to the eye than irregular pieces. But how vegetables are sliced, diced or chopped will also affect a recipe's taste and texture. Thick slices or large dice of onion, for example, retain more of a presence in a finished dish, while finely chopped onion virtually dissolves into the other ingredients, suffusing them with its flavor.

Paring tough stalks.
To pare the tough skins from the stems of such vegetables as broccoli or asparagus, use a small, sharp knife to cut parallel to the stem just thickly enough to reveal the more tender flesh beneath. Or use a vegetable peeler.

Peeling thin skins.
To peel the thin skins of such root vegetables as carrots, use a swivel-bladed vegetable peeler, moving the dual-edged blade in both directions along the vegetable for maximum efficiency.

Cutting diagonal slices.
For diagonal slices, steady the vegetable with one hand, tucking in your fingertips for safety. Use a sturdy, sharp knife to cut slices of the desired thickness, holding the blade at a 45-degree angle to the vegetable.

Chopping coarsely.
To chop an onion, first trim off its stem and root ends, then cut it in half vertically. Peel off the skin. From the stem end, cut thick parallel slices toward but not all the way through the root end. Cut crosswise to chop the onion coarsely.

Chopping finely.
For a finer chop, gather a pile of coarsely chopped vegetables. Using a chef's knife, chop the vegetables to the desired fineness, steadying the knife tip with one hand while rocking the blade and arcing it back and forth through the pile.

Cutting uniform dice.
To dice a vegetable, first cut into uniform strips; here, a bell pepper (capsicum) has been halved, stemmed, seeded, deribbed and cut lengthwise into strips ½ inch (12 mm) wide. Hold the strips together and cut crosswise at the same width.

COOKING VEGETABLES

A gallery of basic methods and techniques for cooking vegetables quickly and easily

As the recipes in this book demonstrate, a wide range of cooking methods is used for making vegetable dishes. Those illustrated here are the most basic approaches, useful not only as individual steps in multiple-stage preparations, but also as ends in themselves—yielding simple, unadorned vegetable side dishes.

Whichever method you use, pay careful attention to the cooking time. Many recipes call for vegetables cooked tender yet slightly crisp to the bite. Vegetables to be puréed, on the other hand, must be cooked until soft. The actual cooking time will depend upon the kind of vegetable, its age and size, as well as the size and shape of the pieces into which it has been cut. A sharp knife tip or fork inserted into the vegetable gives some indication of doneness; so do your own teeth, biting carefully into a sample removed from the pot or pan.

BOILING

Boiling vegetable pieces. Bring a large saucepan of water to a boil and then add the vegetables—here, carrots. Continue boiling until the vegetables reach the desired degree of doneness, whether tender-crisp if they will be served in pieces, or softer if they will be puréed.

Cooking whole vegetables. If a recipe calls for vegetables to be cooked whole, select a pan that will hold them comfortably, overlapping as little as possible. Here, for cooking whole asparagus, a wide pan was filled with just enough water to cover the vegetables, then brought to the boil before the vegetables were added.

STEAMING

To assemble a steamer, place a steaming rack inside a saucepan into which it fits snugly. Add water to just below the bottom of the rack, then lay the vegetables on the rack. Cover and bring to a boil, steaming the vegetables to the desired degree of doneness. Or use a 2-piece steaming pot made for this purpose.

BAKING

For recipes requiring basting, such as the baked tomatoes with spinach shown here (recipe on page 40), select a baking dish large enough to allow juices to collect and be spooned up for drizzling over the vegetables.

SAUTÉING

Sautéing in a frying pan.
For rapid sautéing of vegetables, select a wide frying pan with sloping sides that allow moisture to escape rapidly. Heat oil in the pan over medium heat, add the cut-up vegetables and stir vigorously and frequently.

Stir-frying in a wok.
For Chinese-style stir-fried vegetables, use a wok. Its spherical shape allows vegetables to be tossed rapidly for quick cooking. Heat oil in the wok over medium-high heat, add vegetables and use a large spatula or spoon to keep the vegetables in constant motion.

PURÉEING

Using a ricer.
For the lightest and smoothest purées of root vegetables, use a ricer. Put soft-cooked vegetables—here, potatoes—into the hopper; close the handle to force the vegetable through the holes into a mixing bowl. Stir or beat in butter, milk, cream or other liquids, enrichments or seasonings as desired.

Puréeing in a processor.
Put the cooked vegetables into a processor work bowl fitted with the metal blade. Close the lid and pulse to chop coarsely; then add butter, milk, cream or other embellishments and process until smooth. Do not purée potatoes in this way; they will become gummy.

Mediterranean Stuffed Eggplant

LIQUIDS TO ENHANCE FLAVOR AND MOISTURE

Two simple stocks provide flavorful cooking mediums for boiled, steamed, baked, braised or stewed vegetables

Water is the simplest cooking liquid for vegetables. But by substituting another, more flavorful liquid—stock, wine, juice, milk—you can enhance the flavor of the vegetables.

Stock complements vegetables particularly well, and one made from vegetables contributes its own subtle blend of flavors. A chicken stock adds more richness; yet unlike meat or seafood stock, it is mild and won't overwhelm the taste of the vegetable.

Vegetable Stock

A delicately flavored stock for cooking and basting vegetables. Freeze in small containers to defrost as needed.

4 qt (4 l) water
2 carrots, peeled and cut into pieces
4 celery stalks, without leaves, cut into pieces
1 clove garlic, cut in half
1 yellow onion, cut into quarters
2 tomatoes, cut into quarters
5 fresh parsley sprigs
1 teaspoon whole peppercorns
1 bay leaf
salt

Place the water in a large pot and bring to a boil over high heat. Reduce the heat to medium and add the carrots, celery, garlic, onion, tomatoes, parsley, peppercorns and bay leaf. Simmer gently, uncovered, for 1 hour.

Season to taste with salt. Strain through a fine sieve and let cool. The stock may be covered and refrigerated for up to 1 week, or frozen for up to 2 months.

Makes about 3 qt (3 l)

1. Filling the stockpot.
Bring water to a boil in a large pot. Reduce the heat and add aromatic vegetables—onions, carrots, celery, tomatoes—and seasonings. Simmer, uncovered, for 1 hour.

2. Straining the stock.
Season the vegetable stock to taste with salt. Strain the stock into a bowl and discard the solids. Let the stock cool.

Chicken Stock

A well-seasoned stock that enhances the natural flavor of vegetables and imparts a rich quality to all vegetable dishes. Store the stock in small containers in the freezer to defrost as needed for poaching and basting. The cooked chicken can be boned and used for chicken salad, curry dishes, hash or sandwiches. Or serve the whole chicken with the vegetables from the stock.

1 chicken, about 3½ lb (1.75 kg)
juice of 1 lemon
2 celery stalks, without leaves, cut into pieces
2 carrots, peeled and cut into pieces
1 yellow onion, cut into quarters
1 bay leaf
1 teaspoon dried sage
1 teaspoon whole peppercorns
salt

Remove the excess fat from the chicken cavity. Place the chicken in a large pot and add water to cover. Bring to a boil over high heat, then reduce the heat to medium-low. Skim off any scum or froth as it forms on the surface.

Add the lemon juice, celery, carrots, onion, bay leaf, sage and peppercorns. Cover and cook gently until the chicken is tender, about 1 hour. Add water as needed to keep the chicken covered. After 45 minutes of cooking, season to taste with salt.

Transfer the chicken to a plate and set aside for other uses. Strain the stock through a fine sieve and let cool. Cover and refrigerate.

When the stock is cold, skim off the fat and discard. The stock will keep refrigerated for up to 1 week or frozen for up to 2 months.

Makes about 3½ qt (3.5 l)

1. Filling the stockpot.
In a large stockpot, place a whole chicken. Add cold water to cover completely.

2. Skimming the stock.
Bring the liquid to a boil while regularly skimming off froth and scum from the surface with a skimmer. When the stock gently boils, reduce the heat, add seasonings, cover and simmer gently about 1 hour.

3. Straining and degreasing.
Remove the chicken and pour the stock through a fine sieve into a bowl. Let cool to room temperature, then cover and refrigerate. Using a large spoon, skim the solidified fat from its surface.

Basic Sauces

Quickly prepared sauces add extra flavor and color to cooked vegetables

Any of the basic methods of cooking vegetables shown on pages 10–11 can be simply embellished by the addition of one of the sauces on these pages, to yield a side dish that shows off fresh seasonal vegetables at their best.

   But don't limit yourself to these three sauces alone. Olive oil or melted butter—with or without lemon juice or other seasonings—subtly highlights cooked vegetables. Feel free to try other sauces or seasonings from this book as well, such as mustard cream (page 44) or vinaigrette (page 43); or let these examples inspire your own elaborations.

Tomato Sauce

An excellent companion to stuffed vegetables such as stuffed mushrooms with vermouth (recipe on page 25) and vegetable puddings such as corn pudding (page 55). It is also delicious spooned over steamed green beans or quickly sautéed zucchini (courgettes) or tossed with pasta. You will want to have some of this easy-to-make sauce on hand at all times. It can be kept loosely covered in the refrigerator for 4 or 5 days. Serve the sauce hot or at room temperature.

2 tablespoons olive oil
1 clove garlic, cut in half
6 plum (Roma) tomatoes, halved lengthwise
1 teaspoon dried oregano
½ teaspoon dried mint

Warm the oil in a small sauté pan over medium heat. Add the garlic, tomatoes, oregano and mint. Cover and cook for 5 minutes.

   Uncover and break up the tomatoes with a wooden spoon. Stir to mix well. Re-cover and simmer over low heat for 10 minutes.

   Using a wooden spoon, force the tomato mixture through a sieve set over a small bowl. If serving hot, reheat gently.

   Makes about 1 cup (8 fl oz/250 ml)

Tomato Sauce

Béchamel Sauce

This classic sauce, sometimes simply called white sauce, adds a rich and creamy quality to a variety of vegetable dishes. It can be spooned over hot cooked vegetables just before serving, or mixed with them to make an easy yet elegant creamed vegetable course. To turn the creamed vegetables into a gratin, place in a baking dish, top with cheese and then bake in the oven until golden. Or prepare the gratin with a cheese sauce by whisking ½ cup (2 oz/60 g) freshly grated Parmesan, Gruyère or other cheese into the finished béchamel sauce. If a lighter sauce is desired, substitute chicken stock for part of the milk.

3 tablespoons unsalted butter
3 tablespoons all-purpose (plain) flour
1 teaspoon paprika
1 bay leaf
2 cups (16 fl oz/500 ml) milk, heated, or 1 cup
  (8 fl oz/250 ml) each milk and chicken stock, heated
salt and freshly ground white pepper

Melt the butter gently in a saucepan over medium heat. Stir in the flour and cook, stirring, until blended, 1 minute. Add the paprika and bay leaf.

Gradually add the milk or milk and stock, stirring constantly with a small whisk. Continue to whisk over low heat until the sauce is smooth and slightly thickened, 4–5 minutes. Season to taste with salt and white pepper.

Raise the heat to medium and simmer to blend the flavors, 2–3 minutes. Discard the bay leaf before using.

*Makes about 2 cups
(16 fl oz/500 ml)*

Caper Sauce

This is a marvelous sauce for cold vegetables such as carrots and cauliflower, both raw and steamed. It is also good on cooked green beans, asparagus or artichokes.

2 tablespoons well-drained capers, chopped
2 tablespoons chopped fresh parsley
2 tablespoons chopped green (spring) onions, including
  green tops
⅓ cup (3 fl oz/80 ml) dry white wine
juice of ½ lemon
1 cup (8 fl oz/250 ml) mayonnaise
salt and freshly ground pepper

Place the capers, parsley, green onions, wine and lemon juice in a small saucepan. Cook over high heat, stirring, until the wine is reduced by one-fourth, just a few minutes.

Place the mayonnaise in a small bowl and stir in the mixture. Season to taste with salt and pepper.

Makes about 1 cup (8 fl oz/250 ml)

Caper Sauce

Béchamel Sauce

Italian Broccoli with Olives

3 or 4 broccoli stalks, about 1 lb (500 g)
3 tablespoons olive oil
1 tablespoon red wine vinegar
juice of ½ lemon
salt and freshly ground pepper
1 tablespoon well-drained capers
½ cup (2½ oz/75 g) pitted black olives,
  chopped

Here is a simple dish that is ideal as a salad or first course. Serve at room temperature, as the French and Italians do, with pasta and a loaf of good bread.

Split each broccoli stalk lengthwise into thin pieces (the number depends upon the thickness of the stalks). Cut off and discard the coarse leaves and tough lower stems.

Fill a saucepan with just enough water to cover the broccoli once it is added. Bring to a boil. Add the broccoli and cook, uncovered, over high heat until tender but firm, 4–5 minutes. (If cooked quickly, broccoli will retain its bright color.)

Drain and place in a serving dish. Immediately pour the olive oil over the broccoli, add the vinegar and carefully toss. Add the lemon juice and season to taste with salt and pepper. Toss again.

Add the capers and olives, turning the broccoli gently until thoroughly combined. Serve at room temperature.

Serves 4

Baked Onions

4 red (Spanish) onions, unpeeled

4 fresh basil or rosemary sprigs

¼ cup (2 fl oz/60 ml) olive oil

1½ tablespoons balsamic vinegar

1 tablespoon brown sugar

2 tablespoons red wine vinegar

¾ cup (6 fl oz/180 ml) vegetable stock
   or chicken stock (*recipes on pages 12–13*)

salt and freshly ground pepper

The onions must be baked unpeeled; the skins help to retain the full flavor. Once slit after baking, the skins will fall away easily. These onions are an excellent side dish with roasted veal or pork.

Preheat an oven to 375°F (190°C).

Using a sharp knife cut a thin slice off the base of each onion so the onions will sit upright. Cut a thin slice from the top of each onion and then cut a small slit ½ inch (12 mm) deep in the center. Insert a basil or rosemary sprig into each slit. Place the onions in a small baking dish.

In a small bowl stir together the olive oil, balsamic vinegar, sugar, red wine vinegar and stock. Pour into the bottom of the dish and baste the onions. Place in the oven and bake, basting a few times with the dish juices, until the onions are soft when pierced with the point of a sharp knife, 1–1½ hours.

Before serving, split the skins with a sharp knife and remove. Season the onions to taste with salt and pepper.

Serves 4

Creamy Potatoes with Rosemary

3 large baking potatoes, about 1¾ lb
   (875 g) total
2 tablespoons unsalted butter
¼ cup (2 fl oz/60 ml) heavy (double)
   cream, or as needed
2 teaspoons dried rosemary
3 egg yolks
¾ cup (3 oz/90 g) freshly grated Gruyère
   cheese
salt and white pepper
1 cup (8 fl oz/250 ml) tomato sauce
   (recipe on page 14)

Unusual and delicious, this is a wonderful dish for guests because it can be made ahead. If you like, accompany it with baked leeks, mushrooms or puréed spinach.

Preheat an oven to 400°F (200°C). Butter a 1½-qt (1.5-l) soufflé dish and set aside.

Put the potatoes in a heavy saucepan and add water to cover. Bring to a boil over high heat. Reduce the heat to medium, cover and boil gently until tender, 25–30 minutes.

Drain the potatoes and, when cool enough to handle, peel and slice. Put through a food mill or ricer, or mash with a potato masher. Add the butter, cream and rosemary and mix until the potatoes are creamy. Add the egg yolks and stir to combine. Transfer to the prepared dish and fold in all but 2 tablespoons of the cheese and salt and white pepper to taste. Smooth the surface with the back of a spoon. Pour ⅓ cup (3 fl oz/80 ml) of the tomato sauce evenly over the top and sprinkle with the remaining cheese.

Place in the oven and bake until firm and golden brown, about 30 minutes.

Heat the remaining ⅔ cup (5 fl oz/170 ml) tomato sauce and pour into a bowl to pass at the table.

Serves 4

Potato and Carrot Purée

Potatoes are the base of this vegetable purée; you may substitute other vegetables for the carrots, such as broccoli, turnips or cauliflower. Excellent with pork, ham or poultry.

2 tablespoons olive oil

1 large yellow onion, coarsely chopped

2 cloves garlic, cut in half

1 teaspoon dried sage

1 teaspoon dried thyme

3 baking potatoes, about 1½ lb (750 g) total, peeled and coarsely chopped

2 cups (16 fl oz/500 ml) chicken stock (*recipe on page 13*)

4 carrots, peeled and coarsely chopped

salt and freshly ground white pepper

1 cup (8 fl oz/250 ml) heavy (double) cream

Warm the olive oil in a large saucepan over medium heat. Add the onion and sauté until soft, 2–3 minutes.

Stir in the garlic, sage and thyme and cook for 3 minutes longer. Add the potatoes and stir to incorporate thoroughly. Stir in the stock and simmer gently, uncovered, for 15 minutes.

Add the carrots and continue to simmer until the vegetables are tender, about 15 minutes longer.

Remove from the heat. Put the mixture through a ricer or mash it with a potato masher. Transfer to a clean saucepan and season to taste with salt and white pepper.

Slowly stir in the cream and cook over medium heat until the cream is absorbed, 7–8 minutes. Taste and adjust the seasoning. Serve immediately.

Serves 4–6

Stuffed Mushrooms with Vermouth

8 large fresh mushrooms
3 tablespoons olive oil
2 slices cooked ham, finely chopped
2 tablespoons chopped fresh parsley
3 tablespoons fine dried bread crumbs
½ cup (4 fl oz/120 ml) dry vermouth
¼ teaspoon paprika
salt and freshly ground pepper
2 tablespoons pine nuts

These flavorful stuffed mushrooms are good served on toast rounds or with warm tomato sauce (recipe on page 14). They are a particularly appealing accompaniment to baked tomatoes.

*P*reheat an oven to 350°F (180°C).

Remove the stems from the mushrooms. Finely chop the stems and set aside. Pour 1 tablespoon of the olive oil into a baking dish and spread it evenly over the bottom. Place the mushroom caps in the dish, hollow side up, and brush with some of the oil in the dish.

Warm the remaining 2 tablespoons olive oil in a sauté pan over medium heat. Add the ham and cook, stirring, for 2 minutes. Add the mushroom stems and parsley and cook for 1 minute. Stir in the bread crumbs, ¼ cup (2 fl oz/60 ml) of the vermouth and the paprika. Add salt and pepper to taste. Cook for 2 minutes, stirring constantly as the liquid becomes absorbed.

Remove from the heat and fill the mushroom caps with the mixture. Decorate each cap with several pine nuts. Add the remaining ¼ cup (2 fl oz/60 ml) vermouth to the bottom of the dish.

Place in the oven and bake, basting occasionally with the dish juices, until the caps are tender and the stuffing is golden, 15–20 minutes. Serve at room temperature.

Serves 4

Spinach Ring

2 cups (14 oz/440 g) well-drained
   cooked spinach (2–3 bunches)
2 tablespoons unsalted butter
1½ tablespoons all-purpose (plain) flour
salt and freshly ground pepper
½ cup (4 fl oz/125 ml) milk, heated
½ teaspoon paprika
¾ cup (3 oz/90 g) freshly grated
   Parmesan cheese
3 eggs, well beaten

This recipe can be assembled in advance and refrigerated until going into the oven. Red and yellow tomatoes make a colorful garnish. If using a ring mold, try filling the center or surrounding the edges with small new potatoes sautéed with herbs (recipe on page 52).

*P*reheat an oven to 375°F (190°C). Butter a 1½-qt (1.5-l) ring mold or soufflé dish.

Place the spinach in a food processor fitted with the metal blade and purée. Melt 1 tablespoon of the butter in a sauté pan over medium heat. Add the spinach, raise the heat to high and cook, stirring, until all moisture has cooked away, 1–2 minutes. Reduce the heat to medium.

Stir in the flour and salt and pepper to taste. Slowly pour in the warm milk, stirring constantly until smooth and thickened. Cook over low heat, stirring constantly, for 2 minutes. Add the paprika and cook for 4 minutes longer.

Remove from the heat and add ½ cup (2 oz/60 g) of the cheese and the remaining 1 tablespoon butter. Stir in the eggs and pour into the prepared mold or dish. If using a soufflé dish, mound the surface into a dome. Sprinkle the top with the remaining ¼ cup (1 oz/30 g) cheese. Place in a baking pan and pour hot water into the pan to reach halfway up the sides of the mold or dish. Bake until firm and lightly browned, 30–40 minutes.

Remove from the oven and let sit for a few minutes. Run a knife around the edges, then invert onto a serving plate. Serve hot.

Serves 4

Chinese Cabbage
with Sesame Seeds

2 tablespoons sesame seeds
1½ cups (12 fl oz/375 ml) vegetable
  stock (recipe on page 12)
4 green (spring) onions
1 small head Chinese (nappa) cabbage,
  thinly sliced lengthwise and then cut
  in half crosswise
2 tablespoons unsalted butter
½ teaspoon red pepper flakes
salt and freshly ground white pepper

A mild Asian vegetable with pale green leaves, Chinese cabbage is more like a lettuce than a cabbage. It can be used in many different ways: shredded raw in a salad, steamed or stir-fried Chinese style, or stuffed. Here, it is quickly cooked in stock and flavored with toasted sesame seeds. Offer this dish as an accompaniment to roast chicken or glazed tenderloin of pork.

*P*lace the sesame seeds in a small, dry frying pan over medium-low heat and stir until lightly colored, 2–3 minutes. Set aside.

Pour the vegetable stock into a large frying pan over high heat. Boil to reduce and concentrate the stock, 2–3 minutes.

Cut the green onions in half lengthwise and then cut into long, thin strips. Add to the boiling stock. Add the cabbage and reduce the heat to medium. Cook, stirring occasionally, until tender, about 5 minutes. The stock should be almost totally absorbed.

Stir the butter and sesame seeds into the cabbage and season with the red pepper flakes. Add salt and white pepper to taste.

Serves 4

Sweet-and-Sour Cabbage

3 tablespoons unsalted butter

1 yellow onion, chopped

1 large tart green apple such as Granny
    Smith, cored and chopped

3 tablespoons red wine vinegar

salt and freshly ground pepper

4 cups (¾ lb/375 g) chopped red or
    white cabbage, or a mixture of both

¼ cup (2 fl oz/60 ml) chicken stock
    (recipe on page 13)

2 tablespoons red currant jelly

*This well-seasoned dish goes nicely with sausages, baked ham,
and pork dishes. The sweet-and-sour flavors should be carefully
balanced. Before chopping the cabbage, cut it into quarters,
discard the tough outer leaves, and cut out the hard central core.*

Melt the butter in a large saucepan over medium heat. Add
the onion and cook, stirring, for 2 minutes. Add the apple
and vinegar and season to taste with salt and pepper. Add
the cabbage and stir to mix well. Cover and cook over
medium heat for 10 minutes.

In a small bowl mix together the chicken stock and jelly.
Stir into the cabbage. Re-cover and cook until tender, about
10 minutes.

Taste and add more salt, pepper, jelly and/or vinegar as
needed for a good sweet-sour balance.

Serves 4

Red Bell Peppers with Polenta

4½ cups (36 fl oz/1.1 l) water

½ teaspoon salt

½ cup (3 oz/90 g) polenta or coarse-
   grind yellow cornmeal

2 large red bell peppers (capsicums)

2 tablespoons olive oil

2 large ripe tomatoes, thinly sliced

1 teaspoon dried oregano

salt and freshly ground pepper

1 cup (8 fl oz/250 ml) vegetable stock
   (recipe on page 12)

1 cup (4 oz/125 g) freshly grated
   Gruyère cheese

This marvelous combination of flavors and colors can be prepared in advance. Offer as an accompaniment to sautéed veal or chicken or a fish soup.

Preheat an oven to 375°F (190°C).

Pour 4 cups (32 fl oz/1 l) of the water into a saucepan. Bring to a boil over medium heat and add the salt. Slowly pour in the cornmeal while stirring constantly. Reduce the heat to medium-low and simmer, stirring occasionally. If the cornmeal becomes too stiff, add the remaining ½ cup (4 fl oz/125 ml) water. After about 20 minutes the polenta will be cooked and firm. Set aside.

Cut the peppers in half lengthwise. Remove the seeds and ribs. Cut a thin slice from the rounded side of each half so it will sit upright. Place hollow-side up in a baking dish.

Fill each pepper half with one-fourth of the polenta. Drizzle the oil evenly into the dish. Add the tomatoes to the dish and sprinkle the oregano and salt and pepper to taste over them. Pour in ½ cup (4 fl oz/125 ml) of the stock.

Place in the oven and bake until the peppers are tender, about 40 minutes. During baking, stir and mash the tomatoes with a spoon and baste the peppers with the dish juices several times. After the first 20 minutes of baking, pour in the remaining ½ cup (4 fl oz/125 ml) stock.

When the peppers are tender, sprinkle the cheese evenly over the tops and bake until the cheese melts, about 5 minutes. Spoon the sauce from the dish on top.

Serves 4

Minted Green Peas with Hearts of Lettuce

1 cup (8 fl oz/250 ml) vegetable stock
   (recipe on page 12)
2 fresh parsley sprigs
1 bay leaf
1 fresh mint sprig, plus 1 tablespoon
   finely chopped fresh mint
½ teaspoon sugar
2 cups (10 oz/315 g) shelled fresh peas
   or thawed, frozen peas
2 hearts of butter lettuce
2 tablespoons unsalted butter
salt and freshly ground white pepper

A thoroughly satisfying vegetable dish, especially when made with fresh summer peas and tender hearts of lettuce, unadorned except for butter to enhance the fresh flavors. Excellent with lamb chops.

❋

*P*our the stock into a frying pan and bring to a boil over medium heat.

Meanwhile, gather the parsley sprigs, bay leaf and mint sprig into a bouquet and tie together with kitchen string. Add the bouquet, sugar, peas and hearts of lettuce to the boiling stock. Simmer, uncovered, until the peas are almost tender, 4–5 minutes.

Pour off all but ¼ cup (2 fl oz/60 ml) of the stock. Add the butter and salt and white pepper to taste. Cook, stirring, over medium heat for 2 minutes. Discard the bouquet. Cut the lettuce hearts in half.

Transfer to a bowl and sprinkle with the chopped mint.

Serves 4

Baked Artichokes with Mushroom Stuffing

4 artichokes

juice of 1 lemon

3 tablespoons olive oil

2 cloves garlic, chopped

2 shallots, chopped

½ cup (2 oz/60 g) chopped fresh mushrooms

3 tablespoons chopped fresh parsley

1 tablespoon chopped fresh mint

salt and freshly ground pepper

⅓ cup (1½ oz/45 g) fine dried bread crumbs

4 slices bacon

2 cups (16 fl oz/500 ml) chicken stock, heated (*recipe on page 13*)

These stuffed artichokes can be assembled in advance and baked just before serving. The bacon slices add moisture and flavor.

Preheat an oven to 375°F (190°C).

Half-fill a large saucepan with water and bring to a boil. Cut off the entire stems of the artichokes so they will sit upright. Cut 1 inch (2.5 cm) off the top of each artichoke and remove the tough outer leaves. Place the artichokes upright in the saucepan and add the lemon juice. Reduce the heat to medium, cover and simmer for 15 minutes.

Remove the artichokes and invert to drain well. When cool enough to handle, gently separate the leaves of each artichoke to expose the prickly choke. Using a spoon, scoop out the choke. Set the artichokes aside.

Heat 2 tablespoons of the oil in a frying pan over medium heat. Add the garlic, shallots and mushrooms and sauté until soft, about 2 minutes. Add 2 tablespoons of the parsley, the mint and salt and pepper to taste. Mix in the bread crumbs.

Fill each artichoke with an equal amount of the mixture. Wrap a piece of bacon around the "waist" of each artichoke and secure with a toothpick. Place upright in a baking dish and pour the remaining 1 tablespoon oil around them. Pour in the warm stock. Bake until the artichokes are tender, about 30 minutes.

Remove from the oven and garnish with the remaining 1 tablespoon parsley. Serve hot or at room temperature.

Serves 4

Green Beans with Bacon

½ lb (250 g) small, tender green beans of
    uniform size, trimmed if desired
4 slices bacon, cut into small dice
1 tablespoon unsalted butter
2 green (spring) onions, green tops only,
    finely chopped
freshly ground pepper

*Green beans are good alone or combined with other vegetables in
a vinaigrette sauce. Here, the beans are tossed with crisp bacon
and onions. This is excellent served with roasted or grilled meats
or chicken.*

*F*ill a frying pan with just enough water to cover the beans
once they are added. Bring to a boil. Add the beans, cover
and cook over medium heat until barely tender, 6–7
minutes. Drain well in a colander and set aside.

Cook the bacon in the same pan over medium heat,
stirring constantly, until crisp, 2–4 minutes. Using a slotted
spoon, transfer to paper towels to drain. Pour off the
drippings and wipe out the pan with a paper towel.

Melt the butter in the same pan over medium heat. Add
the onions and sauté gently just until soft, about 1 minute.
Add the beans and toss with the butter. Stir in the bacon
and toss to mix well.

Season to taste with pepper and serve hot or warm.

Serves 3 or 4

Baked Tomatoes with Spinach

2 cups (16 fl oz/500 ml) béchamel sauce
   (recipe on page 15)
6 large ripe tomatoes
2 tablespoons unsalted butter
2 tablespoons chopped green (spring)
   onion, including green tops
2 tablespoons chopped fresh parsley
2 cups (14 oz/440 g) well-drained
   chopped, cooked spinach
   (2–3 bunches)
1 cup (4 oz/120 g) freshly grated
   Parmesan cheese
salt and freshly ground pepper
1 cup (8 fl oz/250 ml) chicken stock
   (recipe on page 13)

An ideal dish for summer meals. Wonderful with a cold soup or with a large salad, cheese, fruit and crusty bread. The extra bonus is that they can be made ahead and served warm or cold.

※

Preheat an oven to 375°F (190°C). Prepare the béchamel sauce and set aside.

Slice off the tops of the tomatoes and scoop out the pulp and seeds. Invert the tomatoes on a dish to drain.

Melt the butter in a frying pan over medium heat. Add the onion and parsley and sauté for 2 minutes. Add the spinach and cook, stirring, until all the liquid evaporates, about 2 minutes.

Slowly add the béchamel sauce, stirring to mix well with the spinach. Stir in ½ cup (2 oz/60 g) of the cheese and season to taste with salt and pepper. Remove from the heat.

Place the tomatoes, hollow side up, in a baking dish. Sprinkle the insides with salt and pepper. Spoon an equal amount of the spinach mixture into each tomato. Pour ½ cup (4 fl oz/125 ml) of the stock around the tomatoes. Place in the oven and bake until soft, about 40 minutes, basting with the dish juices 2 or 3 times during baking. Add the remaining ½ cup (4 fl oz/125 ml) stock to the dish as needed for basting.

Remove from the oven and sprinkle the remaining ½ cup (2 oz/60 g) cheese evenly over the tomato tops. Return to the oven until the cheese is golden, 5–6 minutes.

Serves 6

Asparagus with Vinaigrette Sauce

1 lb (500 g) asparagus
½ cup (4 fl oz/125 ml) olive oil
2 tablespoons chopped shallots
3 tablespoons red wine vinegar
1½ teaspoons Dijon mustard
salt and freshly ground pepper
2 tablespoons chopped fresh parsley
2 hard-cooked egg yolks

Fresh asparagus is especially delicious when served warm with a shallot vinaigrette sauce to heighten its flavor. This elegant preparation is an ideal accompaniment to almost any chicken or veal dish.

Using a sharp knife, cut off the tough ends of the asparagus. Pare the stalks to within about 2 inches (5 cm) of the tips.

Fill a large frying pan or sauté pan with just enough water to cover the asparagus once it is added. Bring to a boil. Add the asparagus, overlapping them as little as possible, and cook, uncovered, over high heat until tender but still quite firm, 3–4 minutes (the amount of time depends upon the thickness of the stalks). Drain well and transfer to a serving plate.

In a small bowl, whisk together the olive oil, shallots, vinegar and mustard. Season to taste with salt and pepper and add the parsley. Spoon the dressing over the warm asparagus. To garnish, using a wooden spoon force the egg yolks through a fine-mesh sieve held over the asparagus.

Serves 4

Kohlrabi with Mustard Cream Sauce

3 cups (24 fl oz/750 ml) vegetable stock
   (recipe on page 12)
1 lb (500 g) kohlrabies
juice of 1 lemon

FOR THE SAUCE:
3 tablespoons unsalted butter
2 shallots, finely chopped
3 tablespoons all-purpose (plain) flour
½ teaspoon paprika
2 cups (16 fl oz/500 ml) milk
1 teaspoon Dijon mustard
3 tablespoons dry vermouth
salt and freshly ground white pepper

¼ cup (1 oz/30 g) fine dried bread
   crumbs
½ cup (2 oz/60 g) freshly grated Gruyère
   cheese

A perfect dish with grilled fish or poultry. This knobby vegetable has a taste similar to that of a turnip and can be substituted for turnips in many dishes. Because of its crisp texture, shredded kohlrabi is ideal in a stir-fry with other vegetables.

Preheat an oven to 375°F (190°C).

Pour the stock into a saucepan and bring to a boil. Meanwhile, peel the kohlrabies and cut crosswise into slices ¾ inch (2 cm) thick. As they are cut, place in a bowl and toss with the lemon juice, to prevent discoloration.

When the stock is boiling, add the kohlrabies. Reduce the heat, cover and simmer until tender, about 10 minutes. Drain and set aside.

Meanwhile, make the sauce. Melt the butter in a saucepan over medium heat. Add the shallots and sauté for 1 minute. Stir in the flour and cook, stirring, until blended, 1 minute. Add the paprika. Gradually add the milk, stirring constantly with a small whisk. Continue to whisk over low heat until the sauce is smooth and slightly thickened, 4–5 minutes. Mix in the mustard and vermouth and season to taste with salt and white pepper. Remove from the heat.

Place the kohlrabies in a baking dish. Spoon the warm sauce over to cover completely. Sprinkle the bread crumbs and cheese over the top. Place in the oven and bake until the sauce bubbles and the top is golden, 15–20 minutes.

Serves 2 or 3

Asparagus with Prosciutto

12 asparagus
4 thin slices prosciutto
2 tablespoons unsalted butter, cut into
  small bits
freshly ground pepper
½ cup (2 oz/60 g) freshly grated
  Parmesan cheese
½ teaspoon paprika
1 lemon, quartered

The prosciutto and cheese heighten the flavor of the fresh asparagus in this classic Italian dish. It can be served as a first course followed by lightly sautéed chicken breasts or veal.

Preheat an oven to 375°F (190°C). Butter a baking dish large enough to hold the asparagus and set aside.

Using a sharp knife, cut off the tough ends of the asparagus. Pare the stalks to within about 2 inches (5 cm) of the tips. Gather the stalks together and trim off the bottoms so all the asparagus are the same length.

Fill a frying pan or sauté pan with just enough water to cover the asparagus once it is added. Bring to a boil. Add the asparagus, overlapping them as little as possible, and cook, uncovered, over high heat until tender but still quite firm, 3–4 minutes (the amount of time depends upon the thickness of the stalks). Drain well.

Divide the asparagus into 4 bundles of 3 stalks each. Wrap 1 prosciutto slice around the center of each bundle. Place the 4 bundles in the prepared dish. Dot with the butter, season to taste with pepper, and sprinkle evenly with the cheese. Place in the oven for 5 minutes to brown the cheese.

Remove from the oven, dust with the paprika and serve hot with the lemon quarters.

Serves 4

Okra with Tomatoes

3 tablespoons olive oil

1 yellow onion, chopped

1 clove garlic, cut in half

1 teaspoon dried rosemary

1 lb (500 g) okra, stemmed and thinly
sliced crosswise (about 3 cups)

1 cup (8 fl oz/250 ml) tomato sauce
(recipe on page 14)

4 tomatoes, coarsely chopped

1 bay leaf

¼ teaspoon red pepper flakes

salt and freshly ground pepper

2 tablespoons chopped fresh parsley
for garnish

Okra is dearly loved by those who are familiar with it. The fresh tomato sauce gives it a zesty taste. Very good with fried chicken, pan-broiled steak or meat loaf.

Warm the oil in a frying pan over medium heat. Add the onion and sauté until soft, about 2 minutes. Add the garlic and cook until soft, about 1 minute longer. Add the rosemary and okra and stir until coated thoroughly with the oil.

Stir in the tomato sauce. Add the tomatoes, bay leaf and red pepper flakes. Simmer, uncovered, over medium heat until the okra is tender, 10–15 minutes.

Season to taste with salt and pepper. Discard the bay leaf and garlic halves. Serve hot or warm, garnished with the parsley.

Serves 4–6

Leeks with Onions, Shallots and Sausage

2 mild Italian sausages, about ½ lb (250 g) total weight

1 cup (8 fl oz/250 ml) dry white wine

6 medium leeks, 4 inches (10 cm) of white part only, trimmed, carefully washed and cut in half lengthwise

1 cup (8 fl oz/250 ml) chicken stock (*recipe on page 13*)

¼ cup (2 fl oz/60 ml) olive oil

6 small, white boiling onions

6 shallots

2 tablespoons fresh lemon juice

1 teaspoon dried thyme

1 teaspoon dried marjoram

1 bay leaf

salt and freshly ground pepper

1½ teaspoons balsamic vinegar

2 tablespoons finely chopped fresh parsley

An elegant and pleasing dish that makes a light prelude to a meal. Enjoy this appetizer with good bread.

Preheat an oven to 350°F (180°C).

Place the sausages in a baking dish and pour ½ cup (4 fl oz/125 ml) of the wine over them. Place in the oven and bake until brown and cooked through, about 40 minutes, basting a few times with the dish juices.

Meanwhile, place the leeks in a saucepan. Add the chicken stock, the remaining ½ cup (4 fl oz/125 ml) wine, the olive oil, whole onions and shallots, lemon juice, thyme, marjoram, bay leaf and salt and pepper to taste. Bring to a simmer over medium heat and cook, uncovered, until tender, 20–25 minutes. Remove from the heat and let cool. Stir in the balsamic vinegar.

Remove the sausages, discarding the cooking liquid. Thinly slice them lengthwise. Add to the leeks and mix well. Just before serving, remove the bay leaf. Place the leeks, onions, shallots, sausage and their marinade in a serving dish. Sprinkle with the parsley and serve.

Serves 4 as an appetizer

New Potatoes with Lemon Butter and Fresh Herbs

16 small new potatoes, 1–1½ lb
(500–750 g)
2 tablespoons unsalted butter
3 tablespoons olive oil
grated zest and juice of 1 lemon
1 tablespoon chopped fresh chives
1 tablespoon chopped fresh basil
1 tablespoon chopped fresh parsley
salt and freshly ground pepper

For an attractive presentation, use a paring knife to remove a band of skin around the middle of each potato before cooking; leave the rest of the skin intact. The green herbs add zest and color to the potatoes. These will enhance grilled meat and fish, or serve them with the spinach ring (recipe on page 26).

*A*rrange the unpeeled potatoes in a single layer in a large frying pan. Add water to cover and place over high heat. Bring to a boil, reduce the heat to low, cover and simmer until tender but still firm, 10–12 minutes. Drain well.

Warm the butter and olive oil in a frying pan over low heat. Add the lemon zest, chives, basil, parsley, potatoes and salt and pepper to taste. Heat gently, stirring to coat the potatoes on all sides with the butter mixture. Add the lemon juice, stir well and serve immediately.

Serves 4

Corn Pudding

3 eggs

2 cups (12 oz/375 g) fresh corn kernels or drained, canned corn kernels

2 tablespoons chopped green (spring) onion, including green tops

½ cup (2½ oz/75 g) chopped red bell pepper (capsicum)

5 tablespoons all-purpose (plain) flour

salt

½ teaspoon paprika

¼ teaspoon cayenne pepper

¼ cup (2 oz/60 g) unsalted butter, melted

1 cup (8 fl oz/250 ml) half-and-half

This is a delightful summer recipe; you can use fresh corn when in season, but it is also good made with canned corn. To remove the kernels from a fresh ear of corn, hold the ear upright and use a sharp knife to cut the kernels off. The savory pudding goes well with outdoor grilled foods, yet is also excellent on a cold winter day with roast meat or chicken.

Preheat an oven to 350°F (180°C). Butter a 1½-qt (1.5-l) soufflé dish and set aside.

In a large bowl beat the eggs until light and frothy. Stir in the corn, onion and bell pepper.

In a small bowl stir together the flour, salt to taste, paprika and cayenne. Add to the corn mixture, stirring to blend. Stir in the melted butter and the half-and-half and mix well. Pour into the prepared dish and place in a baking pan. Pour hot water into the pan to reach about one-fourth of the way up the sides of the dish.

Place in the oven and bake until the top is golden and a knife inserted in the center comes out clean, about 40 minutes. Let rest for 5 minutes before serving.

Serves 4

Grilled Summer Vegetables

2 green zucchini (courgettes), cut
  lengthwise into 3 slices

2 yellow zucchini, cut lengthwise into
  3 slices

2–4 pattypan squashes, cut in half
  crosswise

2 large ripe tomatoes, cut in half
  crosswise

2 slender (Asian) eggplants (aubergines),
  unpeeled, cut lengthwise into 3 slices

4 green (spring) onions, including green
  tops, all trimmed to the same length,
  or 2 red (Spanish) onions, cut in half
  crosswise

½ cup (1 oz/30 g) chopped fresh basil

FOR THE MARINADE:

½ cup (4 fl oz/125 ml) olive oil

3 tablespoons red wine vinegar

2 tablespoons fresh lemon juice

2 cloves garlic, cut in half

1 tablespoon chopped fresh sage or
  dried sage

3 tablespoons chopped fresh chives
  or mint

salt and freshly ground pepper

*How wonderful it is to find summer's harvest in the markets and
bring it home to prepare on your outdoor grill. These vegetables
are good with fish, chicken or lamb; the marinade can be used on
the fish or meat, too. Increase the vegetables as needed to serve
more guests.*

Place all the vegetables in a large glass or ceramic dish and
sprinkle the basil over them.

To make the marinade, stir together all the ingredients,
including salt and pepper to taste. Pour the marinade evenly
over the vegetables and let stand at room temperature for
1 hour, turning the vegetables once.

Prepare a fire in a charcoal grill. Place the vegetables on the
grill rack over the hot coals and grill until tender, 3–6
minutes on each side, depending upon the vegetable.
Alternatively, preheat a broiler (griller). Arrange the
vegetables in a shallow flameproof pan and place under the
broiler 3–4 inches (7.5–10 cm) from the heat. Broil (grill)
3–5 minutes on each side, depending upon the vegetable.

Serves 4

Mediterranean Stuffed Eggplant

2 globe eggplants (aubergines), about
  1 lb (500 g) each
salt
4 tablespoons (2 fl oz/60 ml) olive oil
1 cup (6 oz/180 g) ground (minced)
  ham or veal
1 cup (4 oz/125 g) chopped red
  (Spanish) onion
2 cloves garlic, cut in half
4 ripe tomatoes, thinly sliced
2 cups (16 fl oz/500 ml) vegetable stock
  (recipe on page 12)
1 cup (6 oz/185 g) Arborio or other
  short-grain rice
1 teaspoon dried marjoram
1 teaspoon dried thyme
salt and freshly ground pepper
2 tablespoons chopped fresh parsley

*P*reheat an oven to 350°F (180°C).

Using a sharp knife, cut the eggplants in half lengthwise. Sprinkle the cut sides with salt and place cut-side down in a colander to drain for 30 minutes.

Warm 2 tablespoons of the oil in a large frying pan over medium heat. Add the ham or veal and sauté for 3–4 minutes. Add the onion and garlic and sauté until soft, 2–3 minutes. Stir in 2 of the sliced tomatoes and ½ cup (4 fl oz/125 ml) of the stock. Cover and simmer over low heat for 5 minutes.

Meanwhile, rinse the eggplant halves under cold water. Scoop out most of the flesh, leaving shells about 1 inch (2.5 cm) thick. Coarsely chop the flesh and stir into the tomato mixture.

Add the rice, marjoram, thyme and 1 cup (8 fl oz/250 ml) of the stock, stirring to mix well. Cover and simmer over medium heat for 15 minutes, stirring a few times to prevent sticking. Discard the garlic halves. Season to taste with salt and pepper.

Fill each eggplant shell with one-fourth of the stuffing. Place in a baking dish. Pour the remaining 2 tablespoons oil around the eggplants. Place the remaining 2 sliced tomatoes around the eggplants and pour in the remaining ½ cup (4 fl oz/125 ml) stock.

Place in the oven and bake until the eggplants are tender, 40–45 minutes. During baking, stir and mash the tomatoes with a spoon and baste the eggplants with the tomato-stock mixture several times.

Place the eggplants on a platter and sprinkle with the parsley. Serve hot with the sauce from the dish spooned over the top.

Serves 4

Chinese-Style Vegetables

¼ cup (2 fl oz/60 ml) cold-pressed
    sesame oil or safflower oil
3 tender celery stalks, trimmed and cut
    on the diagonal
½ lb (250 g) green beans, trimmed and
    cut on the diagonal
6 cauliflower florets, cut on the diagonal
6 broccoli florets, cut on the diagonal
1 small bok choy, leaves cut into long,
    thin slivers
1 cup (8 fl oz/250 ml) vegetable stock,
    heated *(recipe on page 12)*
1 tablespoon soy sauce
½ teaspoon red pepper flakes
½ cup (3 oz/90 g) pine nuts or almonds

A crisp and appealing dish of fresh green and white vegetables, with the unexpected surprise of pine nuts or almonds. All of the vegetables must be sliced and ready before starting the cooking process. This stir-fry is good with steamed rice mixed with finely grated lemon zest.

W arm the oil in a large wok or frying pan over medium heat. Add the celery, beans, cauliflower, broccoli and bok choy and stir until coated with the oil. Raise the heat to high and add ½ cup (4 fl oz/125 ml) of the stock, the soy sauce and red pepper flakes. Stir constantly until the vegetables are barely tender, 2–4 minutes, depending upon how well done you prefer them. When the stock evaporates, add only enough of the remaining stock as needed to prevent sticking.

Taste for seasoning and adjust with more soy sauce and/or pepper flakes. Stir in the pine nuts or almonds (if using almonds, coarsely chop them) and serve.

Serves 4

Baked Beets with Orange

12 small, young beets (beetroots) with
  greens attached
½ cup (4 fl oz/125 ml) water
½ cup (4 fl oz/125 ml) olive oil
¼ cup (2 fl oz/60 ml) red wine vinegar
¼ cup (2 fl oz/60 ml) fresh orange juice
3 tablespoons chopped fresh tarragon
salt and freshly ground pepper

A simple dish that requires little time in the kitchen. It is marvelous served at room temperature with grilled fish. The smaller the beets, the better the dish will be. If fresh tarragon isn't available, substitute fresh parsley or chives.

*P*reheat an oven to 350°F (180°C).

Cut off the greens from the beets, leaving about ½ inch (12 mm) of the stems. Discard the tough, damaged outer leaves. Thoroughly wash the beets and greens. Chop the greens coarsely. Place the whole beets and the greens in a baking dish with a lid. Add the water, cover the dish and place in the oven. Bake until the beets are tender, 40–50 minutes (the amount of time will depend upon the size of the beets).

Remove from the oven and set aside to cool. Trim off the stem and root ends. Peel the beets; the skins will slip off easily. Slice the beets thinly and place on a serving plate. Using a slotted spoon, transfer the greens to the plate and arrange around the beets.

In a small bowl stir together the oil, vinegar, orange juice and 2 tablespoons of the tarragon. Season to taste with salt and pepper.

Pour the dressing evenly over the beets and greens. Garnish with the remaining 1 tablespoon tarragon.

Serves 4

Green Beans with Celery and Water Chestnuts

½ lb (250 g) small, tender green beans of uniform size, trimmed and cut in half lengthwise
4 large, tender inner celery stalks, trimmed and thinly sliced crosswise
½ cup (3 oz/90 g) thinly sliced water chestnuts
½ cup (4 fl oz/125 ml) olive oil
3 tablespoons red wine vinegar
few drops of soy sauce
1 tablespoon heavy (double) cream
salt and freshly ground pepper

Fresh green beans cooked until barely tender and then tossed with crisp celery and water chestnuts is an especially refreshing combination of flavors and textures. Good with roast spring lamb or roast chicken with rosemary.

*F*ill a saucepan with just enough water to cover the beans once they are added. Bring to a boil. Add the beans, cover and cook over medium heat until barely tender, 6–7 minutes. Drain the beans.

Combine the beans, celery and water chestnuts in a serving bowl.

In a small bowl whisk together the olive oil, vinegar, soy sauce, cream and salt and pepper to taste. Pour the dressing over the vegetables and toss well. Serve at room temperature.

Serves 4

Summer Ratatouille

1 small globe eggplant (aubergine),
   about 1 lb (500 g)
salt
¼ cup (2 fl oz/60 ml) olive oil
1 red (Spanish) onion, thinly sliced
1 yellow or red bell pepper (capsicum),
   seeded, deribbed and sliced lengthwise
2 cloves garlic, cut in half
2 large ripe tomatoes, sliced
1 teaspoon dried thyme
1 teaspoon dried oregano
¼ cup (2 fl oz/60 ml) vegetable stock
   (recipe on page 12)
freshly ground pepper
2 tablespoons chopped fresh parsley
   or basil

A summer dish of fresh vegetables slowly cooked in fragrant olive oil. If possible, make it a day in advance of serving to allow the flavors to meld. This classic French dish can be served at room temperature as a salad, warm as an appetizer with a few drops of vinegar and a scattering of capers, or hot as a vegetable with cold sliced lamb or chicken and garlic bread.

Cut the unpeeled eggplant lengthwise into quarters, then cut each quarter into long, thin strips. Place in a colander, sprinkle with salt and allow to drain for 30 minutes.

Heat the olive oil in a large frying pan over medium heat. Add the onion and sauté until soft, about 5 minutes. Add the bell pepper, garlic and tomatoes and stir well. Mix in the thyme and oregano.

Meanwhile, rinse the eggplant under cold water and dry well with paper towels. Add to the pan along with the stock. Cover and simmer over low heat, stirring occasionally to prevent sticking, until soft, 20–30 minutes.

Discard the garlic halves. Season to taste with salt and pepper. Transfer to a serving dish and sprinkle with the parsley or basil. Serve hot, warm or at room temperature.

Serves 4

Cucumbers and Green Peas

1 cucumber

1½ cups (12 fl oz/375 ml) vegetable
   stock (recipe on page 12)

1 cup (5 oz/155 g) fresh shelled peas

¼ cup (2 fl oz/60 ml) heavy (double)
   cream

1 tablespoon unsalted butter

4 tablespoons chopped fresh parsley

salt and freshly ground pepper

Cooked cucumbers complement dishes such as roast veal, breaded veal cutlets or sautéed chicken breasts. Frozen peas may also be used, but be sure to thaw them; cooking time will also be shorter.

Using a sharp knife or vegetable peeler, cut strips of the peel from the cucumber to give it a striped appearance. Cut the cucumber in half lengthwise. Using a spoon, scoop out the seeds. Then cut the cucumber halves crosswise into slices ⅜ inch (1 cm) thick.

Pour the stock into a frying pan and bring to a boil. Add the cucumber slices and peas and cook, uncovered, over medium heat until nearly tender, about 4 minutes.

Remove from the heat and pour off the stock into a bowl. Set the pan with the vegetables aside. Measure ½ cup (4 fl oz/125 ml) of the stock and pour it into a small saucepan. Stir in the cream and bring to a boil over high heat. Cook, uncovered, until the sauce thickens, 3–4 minutes.

Add the butter to the pan holding the peas and cucumbers. Place over medium heat to melt the butter. Add the parsley and cook, stirring, for 1 minute. Add the sauce and simmer to blend the flavors, 3–4 minutes. Season to taste with salt and pepper and serve.

Serves 4

Lima Beans with Ham

1 lean ham hock, about 1¼ lb (625 g)

2 tablespoons unsalted butter

1 teaspoon dried sage

2 tablespoons chopped fresh parsley

½ tomato, coarsely chopped

1 cup (8 fl oz/250 ml) chicken stock
  (*recipe on page 13*)

2 carrots, peeled and cut into pieces
  2 inches (5 cm) long and ½ inch
  (12 mm) thick

6 small, white boiling onions, cut in half

2 cups (10 oz/315 g) freshly shelled or
  thawed, frozen lima beans

salt and freshly ground pepper

This dish is good with a simple pasta or with broiled fish.

Cut the meat from the ham hock. Trim off excess fat, then cut the meat into strips 2 inches (5 cm) long and ½ inch (12 mm) thick.

Melt the butter in a frying pan over medium heat. Add the ham and sauté for 4 minutes, stirring to brown on all sides. Stir in the sage and parsley. Add the tomato, pour in the stock and stir well. Cook for 5 minutes, stirring constantly.

Add the carrots and onions and stir well. Bring to a boil and add the lima beans. Reduce the heat to low, cover and simmer for 15 minutes.

Uncover, season to taste with salt and pepper, and continue to cook over medium-high heat until all the vegetables are tender, about 5 minutes longer.

Serves 4

Stir-Fried Vegetables with Shrimp

½ lb (250 g) fresh shrimp (prawns), peeled and deveined

1 tablespoon soy sauce

2 tablespoons dry sherry

10 snow peas (mangetouts)

4 green (spring) onions

2 small, slender (Asian) Japanese eggplants (aubergines), about ¼ lb (125 g) each

¼ cup (2 fl oz/60 ml) cold-pressed sesame oil or safflower oil

2 tablespoons chopped fresh ginger

2 cloves garlic, cut in half

1 cup (8 fl oz/250 ml) vegetable stock, heated (*recipe on page 12*)

salt and freshly ground pepper

½ cup (3 oz/90 g) water chestnuts, cut in half horizontally

This colorful mix of vegetables and shellfish is a meal in itself. It needs only thin noodles and a dessert of fruit ice.

*I*f the shrimp are large, cut them in half lengthwise. Place in a small bowl with the soy sauce and sherry and mix well.

Cut the snow peas on the diagonal into thin strips. Trim the green onions so each onion is 6 inches (15 cm) long and slice lengthwise into thin slivers. Cut the unpeeled eggplants lengthwise into thin slices, then cut into thin strips 4 inches (10 cm) long. Set the vegetables aside.

Warm the oil in a wok or frying pan over high heat. Add the ginger and garlic and cook for 30 seconds. Add the snow peas, onions and eggplant and rapidly toss for 1 minute. Pour in ½ cup (4 fl oz/125 ml) of the warm stock and add the shrimp with their marinade. Toss and cook for 1 minute. Season to taste with salt and pepper. Add the water chestnuts and rapidly toss for 2 minutes. Add the remaining ½ cup (4 fl oz/125 ml) stock and cook, stirring constantly, until the sauce reduces and thickens, about 2 minutes. Discard the garlic and serve immediately.

Serves 3 or 4

Baked Winter Squash

1 small winter squash, 1½–2 lb
   (750 g–1 kg)
1 cup (8 fl oz/250 ml) vegetable stock
   (recipe on page 12)
4 tablespoons (2 oz/60 g) unsalted butter
½ yellow onion, finely chopped
3 tablespoons chopped fresh parsley
1 teaspoon dried marjoram
2 egg yolks
¼ cup (2 fl oz/60 ml) heavy (double)
   cream
¼ cup (1 oz/30 g) freshly grated
   Parmesan cheese
salt and freshly ground pepper

Use any flavorful, small winter squash, such as Danish, buttercup, butternut or pumpkin, to make this superb accompaniment to roast pork, chicken or turkey. Some squashes will have more pulp than others, in which case you may need to use both shells for serving.

Preheat an oven to 375°F (190°C).

Cut the squash in half lengthwise. Place cut-side down in a baking dish. Pour the stock into the dish. Place in the oven and bake until tender, about 45 minutes. To test, pierce the flesh with a fork.

In a frying pan melt 2 tablespoons of the butter over medium heat. Add the onion and stir until soft, about 2 minutes. Add 2 tablespoons of the parsley and the marjoram and stir for 1 minute. Remove from the heat and set aside.

Scoop out and discard the seeds and fibers from the baked squash halves. Scoop out the pulp, reserving one of the squash shells. Place the pulp in a food processor fitted with the metal blade. Add the remaining 2 tablespoons butter and the egg yolks and process to blend. Add the cream, cheese and reserved onion and again process to blend. Season to taste with salt and pepper. Spoon the squash mixture evenly into the squash shell and place in a baking dish. Bake until the top is golden, 15–20 minutes.

Sprinkle the remaining 1 tablespoon parsley over the top and serve hot, spooned directly from the shell.

Serves 4

Stuffed Swiss Chard

1 bunch Swiss chard

1 cup (8 fl oz/250 ml) tomato sauce
  (recipe on page 14)

1 cup (8 fl oz/250 ml) dry white wine or
  chicken stock (recipe on page 13)

3 tablespoons olive oil

½ yellow onion, chopped

½ cup (2½ oz/75 g) chopped celery

8 fresh mushrooms, chopped

1 clove garlic, chopped

3 tablespoons chopped fresh parsley

½ cup (3 oz/90 g) ground (minced)
  ham, veal or chicken

salt and freshly ground pepper

1 egg, slightly beaten

Here, only the leaves of Swiss chard are used. The Italians also use the stalks alone, which they bake with Parmesan cheese.

Cut off the lower stems of the Swiss chard leaves; discard any discolored leaves. You will need 8 large leaves. Fill a large frying pan with water and bring to a boil. Add the leaves, reduce the heat and simmer, uncovered, just until wilted, 2–3 minutes. Drain and place under cold running water; drain again and place on paper towels to absorb excess moisture. Cut away any hard stem portions. Set the leaves aside.

In the same frying pan, make the tomato sauce. Once the sauce is sieved, return it to the pan and add the wine or stock. Simmer, uncovered, to blend the flavors, 5–6 minutes. Set aside.

In another frying pan warm the oil over medium heat. Add the onion and celery and sauté for 2 minutes. Add the mushrooms, garlic and 2 tablespoons of the parsley and sauté for 2–3 minutes. Stir in the meat and cook for 3 minutes. Season to taste with salt and pepper. Cool briefly.

Mix in the egg. Spoon an equal amount of the meat mixture into the center of each leaf. Fold the sides in toward the center, then fold in the ends, overlapping them to enclose the filling completely and forming a small, neat package.

Arrange the filled leaves, seam side down, in the pan containing the sauce. Cover, bring to a boil, reduce the heat and simmer until the filling is cooked, about 20 minutes.

To serve, place 2 chard packages on each plate. Spoon on tomato sauce and garnish with the remaining parsley. Serve at once. Pass the remaining sauce in a bowl on the side.

Serves 4

Rutabaga with Apples

2 rutabagas (swedes), about 1½ lb
   (750 g) total, peeled and thinly sliced
2 tart apples, peeled, cored and thinly
   sliced
½ cup (4 fl oz/125 ml) fresh orange juice
2 tablespoons unsalted butter
salt and freshly ground white pepper

Part wild cabbage, part wild turnip, with a distinctive cabbagelike flavor, the rutabaga takes on a pretty yellow when cooked. This colorful purée has an affinity for game birds and turkey, as well as roast goose and chicken. Any firm, tart apple such as Granny Smith will work for this recipe. If you like, reserve a few apple slices for garnish.

*P*lace the rutabaga slices in a large frying pan, overlapping them as little as possible. Add water just to cover and bring to a boil over high heat. Cover, reduce the heat to low and simmer until tender, 10–15 minutes. Drain in a colander and set aside.

Place the apples in the same frying pan, overlapping them as little as possible. Add the orange juice. Cover and simmer over medium heat until soft, 5–6 minutes.

Put the apples and their cooking liquid in a food processor fitted with the metal blade. Add the rutabaga slices and purée. Return the purée to the frying pan and heat to serving temperature, stirring well. Add the butter and salt and white pepper to taste.

Transfer to a serving dish and serve immediately.

Serves 4 or 5

Brussels Sprouts and Chestnuts

12 chestnuts

3 cups (24 fl oz/750 ml) chicken stock
(recipe on page 13)

4 small celery stalks, without the leaves

1 strip lemon zest

2 cups (½ lb/250 g) small Brussels
sprouts

juice of ½ lemon

3 tablespoons unsalted butter

salt

⅛ teaspoon cayenne pepper

When winter arrives and the air turns cold, this dish suits the season. Chestnuts, with their slightly sweet taste and crumbly, thick texture, go well with the crisp sprouts. If fresh chestnuts are unavailable, use whole canned chestnuts. A glorious dish with game, duck, goose or poultry.

*U*sing a small, sharp knife, make a gash on the flat side of each chestnut (this will prevent them from bursting). Pour the stock into a saucepan and bring to a boil over high heat. Add the chestnuts, celery and lemon zest. Reduce the heat to low, cover and simmer until the chestnuts are tender, about 30 minutes.

Meanwhile, carefully trim the sprouts, discarding any old or wilted leaves. Place in a large frying pan in a single layer and add water to cover. Bring to a boil over high heat and add the lemon juice. Reduce the heat to medium-low and simmer, uncovered, until barely tender, 8–10 minutes. Drain well and set aside.

Drain the chestnuts well; discard the celery and lemon zest. Using a small, sharp knife, peel the chestnuts while warm, removing both the hard outer shell and the furry inner skin.

Melt the butter in the same large frying pan over medium heat. Add the chestnuts, salt to taste and the cayenne. Sauté to brown and glaze, about 5 minutes. Add the Brussels sprouts and sauté over low heat until heated through and tender, about 5 minutes. Transfer to a serving dish and serve hot.

Serves 4

Celeriac and Potato Purée

1 celeriac (celery root), ¾–1 lb (375–500 g)
juice of 1 lemon
2½ cups (20 fl oz/625 ml) chicken stock
   (recipe on page 13)
3 baking potatoes, peeled
3 tablespoons unsalted butter
½ cup (4 fl oz/125 ml) milk, heated
salt and freshly ground white pepper
1 tablespoon chopped fresh parsley

Celeriac is also called celery root or celery knob and has all the fresh, appealing flavor of celery. It can be grated raw into salads or used for savory soups and purées. This purée goes well with game or grilled meats. Lemon zest makes a nice extra touch.

*P*eel the celeriac and cut it into slices ½ inch (12 mm) thick. Place in a bowl and add the lemon juice. Immediately toss to prevent the slices from turning brown.

Pour the stock into a saucepan and add the celeriac slices. Bring to a boil over high heat. Reduce the heat to low, cover and simmer until tender, about 15 minutes. Drain well in a colander, reserving the cooking liquid.

Put the potatoes in the same saucepan, add water to cover and bring to a boil over high heat. Lower the heat, cover and simmer until tender, about 30 minutes. Drain well.

Put the celeriac and potatoes through a food mill or mash with a potato masher. Transfer to a saucepan over medium heat. Mix in the butter and then gradually add the warm milk, stirring, until the purée is smooth. If the purée is too thick, thin with some of the reserved cooking liquid. Season to taste with salt and white pepper.

Transfer to a serving dish and garnish with the parsley. Serve hot.

Serves 4

Baked Acorn Squash with Chutney

2 acorn squashes
1 cup (8 fl oz/250 ml) chicken stock
   (recipe on page 13)
3 tablespoons unsalted butter
3 tablespoons brown sugar
1 teaspoon ground ginger
¼ teaspoon freshly grated nutmeg
salt and freshly ground pepper
4 tablespoons (3 oz/90 g) apricot or
   plum chutney

Acorn squash may be used in place of pumpkin in most recipes. This treatment of the squash goes well with roast lamb or chicken. Or try it with simply cooked fillet of sole or shrimp (prawns).

Preheat an oven to 350°F (180°C).

Cut each squash in half lengthwise. Scrape out the seeds and fibers and discard. Place cut-side down in a baking dish. Pour the stock into the dish. Place in the oven and bake for 20 minutes.

Meanwhile, in a small ovenproof bowl, combine the butter, sugar, ginger and nutmeg. Place in the oven for a few minutes to melt the butter and sugar.

Remove the squash from the oven. Turn skin-side down and fill each hollow with 1 tablespoon of the butter-sugar mixture. Season to taste with salt and pepper.

Butter a piece of parchment paper or waxed paper and use it to cover the dish loosely, buttered side down. Return to the oven and bake until the squash is tender, about 30 minutes.

Place 1 tablespoon chutney in each squash half. Serve hot.

Serves 4

Jerusalem Artichoke Gratin

1 lb (500 g) Jerusalem artichokes
3 tablespoons unsalted butter
½ yellow onion, chopped
1 teaspoon dried thyme
1 teaspoon dried sage
3 tablespoons all-purpose (plain) flour
2 cups (16 fl oz/500 ml) milk, heated
salt and freshly ground white pepper
¼ cup (1 oz/30 g) freshly grated
   Parmesan cheese
paprika

A bulbous root with a delicate texture and flavor. Jerusalem artichokes are easier to peel when cooked. This gratinéed dish is excellent with roasted or broiled meats or with veal scaloppine.

Preheat an oven to 400°F (200°C).

Fill a large saucepan with just enough water to cover the Jerusalem artichokes once they are added. Bring to a boil. Add the Jerusalem artichokes and cook, uncovered, over high heat until tender but not mushy, about 15 minutes. Drain well and let cool. Peel and cut into slices ½ inch (12 mm) thick. Place in a bowl and set aside.

Melt the butter in a saucepan over medium heat. Add the onion, thyme and sage and sauté for 2 minutes. Add the flour and cook, stirring, for 1 minute. Slowly add 1 cup (8 fl oz/250 ml) of the warm milk, stirring constantly. As the sauce begins to thicken, slowly stir in the remaining 1 cup (8 fl oz/250 ml) milk. Continue to stir until thickened, 1–2 minutes. Season to taste with salt and pepper.

Mix the sauce with the Jerusalem artichokes and transfer to a 1½-qt (1.5-l) baking dish. Sprinkle with the cheese and dust with paprika. Place in the oven and bake until the sauce bubbles and the cheese is golden, 10–15 minutes.

Serve hot directly from the baking dish.

Serves 4

Celery Hearts and Leeks

2 bunches celery
1¾ lb (875 g) leeks of uniform size
3 cloves garlic
3 tablespoons olive oil
1 teaspoon dried thyme
1–1½ cups (8–12 fl oz/250–375 ml)
   chicken stock (recipe on page 13)
salt and freshly ground white pepper
1 tablespoon chopped fresh parsley

Here is a side dish that complements many meat, chicken or fish main courses. It also makes an ideal first course, as it may be served hot or at room temperature. For an attractive presentation, tie each leek with a piece of its green stem.

*P*reheat an oven to 375°F (190°C).

Remove and discard the tops and tough outer stalks from the celery. Cut each bunch into quarters lengthwise.

Cut off the green tops and root ends from the leeks. Slit each leek lengthwise three-fourths of the way down to the root end. Wash well to remove all sand.

Place the celery, leeks and garlic cloves in a baking dish. Drizzle the olive oil around and over the vegetables and sprinkle with the thyme. Add ½ cup (4 fl oz/125 ml) of the stock to the dish. Oil a piece of parchment paper or waxed paper and use to cover the dish loosely, oiled side down.

Place in the oven and bake for 20 minutes. Remove from the oven, baste with the dish juices and add more stock to the dish as needed. Return to the oven and bake until the vegetables are tender, 20–30 minutes. Baste 2 or 3 times during baking, adding more stock as needed if the vegetables begin to become dry.

Season to taste with salt and white pepper. Garnish with the parsley. Serve hot or at room temperature.

Serves 4

Parsnip and Carrot Fritters

3 parsnips, about ¾ lb (375 g) total
weight
3 carrots, about ¾ lb (375 g) total weight
2 egg yolks
¼ cup (1 oz/30 g) all-purpose (plain)
flour, plus 1–2 tablespoons if needed
1 teaspoon baking powder
salt and freshly ground white pepper
about 15 pecan halves
3 tablespoons unsalted butter
6 fresh parsley sprigs

These make a wonderful accompaniment to roasted pork or baked ham. The vegetables may be puréed a day in advance and refrigerated, then shaped just before cooking. Although most fritters are deep-fried, these are lightly browned in butter.

*P*eel the parsnips and carrots. Cut into 2-inch (5-cm) pieces. Place in a saucepan, add water to cover and place over high heat. Bring to a boil; reduce the heat to medium and simmer, uncovered, until the vegetables are tender, 20–25 minutes. Drain well.

Transfer the parsnips and carrots to a food processor fitted with the metal blade and purée. Add the egg yolks and process for a few seconds, then add the flour, baking powder and salt and white pepper to taste. Process until well mixed. The batter should be fairly stiff; if it is too thin, add 1–2 tablespoons flour.

Using a tablespoon, form the mixture into ovals; you will have about 15 ovals in all. Tuck a pecan half into the center of each oval.

Melt 1 tablespoon of the butter in a frying pan over medium heat. When the butter foams, add some of the fritters and cook until golden brown, about 2 minutes on each side. Transfer to a warmed serving dish and keep warm. Add 1 tablespoon of the remaining butter to the pan and cook more fritters in the same manner. Repeat with the remaining 1 tablespoon butter and fritters.

Garnish with the parsley sprigs and serve hot.

Serves 4–6

Turnip and Pear Purée

6 small, white turnips, peeled and sliced
   crosswise ½ inch (12 mm) thick
2 tablespoons unsalted butter
pinch of sugar
salt
2 ripe brown winter pears, such as Bosc,
   peeled, cored and thinly sliced
   lengthwise
juice of ½ lemon
½ cup (4 fl oz/125 ml) water
freshly ground white pepper
1 tablespoon finely grated orange zest

This is a delicious and unusual combination. The subtle flavor of the pears complements the sharp, peppery taste of the turnips. Serve in winter with roast pork, veal or turkey.

*P*lace the turnip slices in a large frying pan, overlapping them as little as possible. Add water to cover barely, 1 tablespoon of the butter, the sugar and salt to taste. Bring to a boil over medium heat. Reduce the heat to low, cover and simmer until tender, 12–15 minutes.

Meanwhile, place the pears in a small saucepan with the lemon juice and the ½ cup (4 fl oz/125 ml) water. Cover and simmer gently over low heat until soft, 5–6 minutes.

Drain the turnips and pears. Place in a food processor fitted with the metal blade and process until smooth. Transfer to a saucepan and stir over high heat for a few minutes to evaporate any remaining liquid. Add the remaining 1 tablespoon butter and season to taste with salt and white pepper. Stir in the orange zest and transfer to a serving dish. Serve hot.

Serves 4

Cauliflower with Broccoli Purée

8 cups (64 fl oz/2 l) water

1 small cauliflower, about 1 lb (500 g)

2 cups (8 oz/250 g) chopped broccoli florets

2 green (spring) onions, white part only, coarsely chopped

½ cup (4 fl oz/125 ml) heavy (double) cream

½ teaspoon paprika, plus extra paprika for dusting

1 cup (4 oz/120 g) freshly grated Parmesan cheese

An attractive addition to the buffet table, this dish can be prepared in advance. Excellent with chicken and beef.

Preheat an oven to 350°F (180°C).

Pour 6 cups (48 fl oz/1.5 l) of the water into a large saucepan and bring to a boil. Add the cauliflower, stem end down. Cover, reduce the heat to low and simmer for 10 minutes. Turn the cauliflower over, stem end up, and cook until barely tender, about 10 minutes longer. Drain well and set aside.

Pour the remaining 2 cups (16 fl oz/500 ml) water into a frying pan and bring to a boil. Add the broccoli and cook over high heat, uncovered, until barely tender, 3–4 minutes. Drain well.

Transfer the broccoli to a food processor fitted with the metal blade. Add the onions and purée until smooth. Transfer to a bowl. Add the cream, ½ teaspoon paprika and ½ cup (2 oz/60 g) of the cheese and stir to mix well.

Spoon one-half of the broccoli purée over the bottom of a baking dish. Place the whole cauliflower on top, stem side down. Spoon the remaining broccoli purée over the cauliflower. Sprinkle the remaining ½ cup (2 oz/60 g) cheese over the top and dust with paprika. Place in the oven and bake until the sauce is bubbling, 10–15 minutes.

Cut into wedges and serve hot directly from the dish.

Serves 4

Gratin of Yams and Apples

4 yams, 2–2½ lb (1–1.25 kg) total

2 tablespoons unsalted butter

2 green apples, such as Granny Smith,
cored and cut crosswise into slices
¼ inch (6 mm) thick

salt and freshly ground pepper

1 cup (8 fl oz/250 ml) heavy (double)
cream

¼ cup (2 fl oz/60 ml) sweet vermouth

¼ cup (2 fl oz/60 ml) fresh orange juice

½ teaspoon freshly grated nutmeg

½ cup (2 oz/60 g) fine dried bread
crumbs

Easy to make, this gratin is a wonderful accompaniment to pork, ham or turkey for holiday dinners. In the United States, the vegetable labeled "yam" is actually a type of sweet potato. It has sweet, moist, dark orange flesh and reddish skin. Yams are also good sliced and baked with red (Spanish) onion slices.

*P*reheat an oven to 350°F (180°C).

Place the yams in a large saucepan and add water to cover. Bring to a boil over high heat. Reduce the heat to medium-low and simmer, uncovered, until tender, 20–30 minutes. Drain and let cool. Peel and cut crosswise into slices ½ inch (12 mm) thick.

Melt the butter in a frying pan over medium heat. Add the apple slices and sauté until golden, about 3 minutes on each side. Remove from the heat.

Place half of the yam slices in a baking dish and season to taste with salt and pepper. In a small bowl stir together the cream, vermouth, orange juice and nutmeg and pour half of the mixture evenly over the yams in the dish. Cover with the apple slices and then place the remaining yam slices on top. Pour over the remaining cream mixture. Sprinkle the bread crumbs evenly over the top.

Place in the oven and bake until browned and bubbling, about 30 minutes. Serve hot directly from the baking dish.

Serves 4

Braised Fennel

2 fennel bulbs
¼ cup (2 oz/60 g) unsalted butter
juice of 1 lemon
1 cup (8 fl oz/250 ml) chicken stock,
   heated (*recipe on page 13*)
salt and freshly ground white pepper
1 tablespoon finely chopped fresh
   parsley, optional

This easily prepared dish makes a light first course or a luncheon dish with crisp bread. Or serve it as an accompaniment to fish or braised veal.

Trim off any discolored areas of the fennel bulbs. Remove the tough tubular stalks and feathery tops. Cut the bulbs into quarters lengthwise.

   Melt the butter in a large sauté pan or frying pan over medium heat. Add the fennel in a single layer and sauté until golden on both sides, 6–7 minutes.

   Add the lemon juice and then stir in ½ cup (4 fl oz/125 ml) of the warm stock. Using a spoon, baste the fennel with the pan juices. Season to taste with salt and white pepper. Reduce the heat to low, partially cover and simmer until tender but not mushy, 20–25 minutes. During cooking turn the fennel occasionally and add the remaining stock, 2 tablespoons at a time, as needed; the sauce should be syrupy at end of cooking.

   Sprinkle with the parsley, if desired, and serve hot.

Serves 4

Sweet Potato Pudding

3 sweet potatoes, about 1½ lb (750 g) total weight

⅓ cup (3 fl oz/80 ml) heavy (double) cream

4 eggs

3 tablespoons unsalted butter, melted

2 tablespoons bourbon

1½ teaspoons fresh lemon juice

1 tablespoon grated lemon zest

½ teaspoon freshly grated nutmeg

½ teaspoon ground cinnamon

1 teaspoon ground ginger

salt

pecan halves for topping, optional

Serve this spice-laced pudding with soup and a green salad for a winter meal, or with roast turkey or baked ham for a holiday feast. Because it can be prepared in advance and has an appealing golden crust, this dish is ideal for a dinner party with roasted meat or poultry.

*P*reheat an oven to 375°F (190°C). Butter a 1–1½-qt (1–1.5-l) soufflé dish.

Place the unpeeled sweet potatoes in a large saucepan, add cold water to cover and bring to a boil over high heat. Reduce the heat, cover and simmer until tender, 30–40 minutes. Drain and let cool.

Peel the sweet potatoes. Transfer to a food processor fitted with the metal blade and purée. Add the cream, eggs and butter and process to blend. Add the bourbon, lemon juice and zest, nutmeg, cinnamon and ginger and process again to mix. Season to taste with salt and process for a few seconds to blend the ingredients.

Spoon into the prepared dish. Place in a large baking pan and pour in hot water to reach halfway up the sides of the dish. Place in the oven and bake until puffed and golden brown on top, about 40 minutes.

Garnish the top with the pecan halves, if desired. Serve hot directly from the soufflé dish.

Serves 4 or 5

Baked Belgian Endive

4 heads Belgian endive (chicory/witloof)
3 tablespoons unsalted butter, melted
juice of 1 lemon
½ cup (4 fl oz/125 ml) chicken stock
    (recipe on page 13)
salt and freshly ground pepper
paprika
¼ cup (1 oz/30 g) freshly grated Gruyère
    cheese
¼ cup (1 oz/30 g) freshly grated
    Parmesan cheese

There are many delectable ways to cook endive; it doesn't always have to go into the salad bowl. This dish makes an elegant accompaniment to a veal roast or sautéed chicken breasts and is wonderful on its own as a light lunch.

*P*reheat an oven to 375°F (190°C). Trim the endives and remove any damaged leaves.

Pour a little of the melted butter into a baking dish. Add the endive and drizzle the remaining butter over the top. Sprinkle with the lemon juice. Pour the stock into the dish and season the endives with salt and pepper. Butter a piece of parchment paper or waxed paper and use it to cover the dish loosely, buttered side down.

Place in the oven and bake for 20 minutes. Remove the paper and baste the endives with the dish juices. Continue baking until the endives are tender and slightly golden, 20–30 minutes longer.

Dust with paprika and sprinkle with the cheeses. Continue to bake until the cheeses melt and turn golden, 5–6 minutes. Serve hot directly from the dish.

Serves 4

Glossary

The following glossary defines terms specifically as they relate to vegetable cookery, and includes major ingredients and seasonings as well as less well known vegetable varieties.

BASIL
Sweet, spicy herb popular in Italian and French cooking, particularly as a seasoning for **tomatoes** and tomato sauces.

BAY LEAVES
Dried whole leaves of the bay laurel tree. Pungent and spicy, they flavor simmered dishes, marinades and pickling mixtures. The French variety, sometimes available in specialty-food shops, has a milder, sweeter flavor than California bay leaves. Discard the leaves before serving.

BELL PEPPER
Fresh, sweet-fleshed, bell-shaped member of the pepper family. Also known as capsicum. Most common in the unripe green form, although ripened red or yellow varieties are also available. Creamy pale yellow, orange and purple-black types may also be found. To prepare a raw bell pepper, cut it in half lengthwise with a sharp knife. Pull out the stem section from each half, along with the cluster of seeds attached to it. Remove any remaining seeds, along with any thin white membranes, or ribs, to which they are attached. Cut the pepper halves into quarters, strips or thin slices, as called for in the specific recipe.

BOK CHOY
Chinese variety of cabbage with elongated crisp white stalks and dark green leaves, with a refreshing, slightly peppery flavor.

BUTTER, UNSALTED
For the recipes in this book, unsalted butter is preferred. Lacking salt, it allows the cook greater leeway in seasoning recipes to taste.

CAPERS
Small, pickled buds of a bush common to the Mediterranean, used as a savory flavoring or garnish. The salty, sharp-tasting brine may also be used as a seasoning.

CAYENNE PEPPER
Very hot ground spice derived from dried cayenne chili peppers.

CELERIAC
Large, knobby root of a species of celery plant, with a crisp texture and fine flavor closely resembling the familiar stalks. Choose smaller, younger roots, to be peeled and eaten raw or cooked. Also known as celery root.

CHINESE CABBAGE
Asian variety of cabbage with long, mild-flavored, pale green to white, crisp leaves, packed in tight, elongated heads. Also known as nappa cabbage.

BREAD CRUMBS
For good bread crumbs, choose a high-quality, rustic-style loaf with a firm, coarse-textured crumb.

For fresh crumbs, cut away the crusts from the bread and break the bread into coarse chunks. Put them in a food processor fitted with the metal blade or in a blender and process to desired consistency.

For dried crumbs, spread the bread crumbs in a baking pan and leave in an oven set at its lowest temperature until they feel very dry, 30–60 minutes; do not let brown.

CHIVES
Mild, sweet herb with a flavor reminiscent of the **onion,** to which it is related. Although chives are available dried in the herb-and-spice section of a food market, fresh chives possess the best flavor.

CHUTNEY
Refers to any number of spiced East Indian–style relishes or pickles served as condiments with meals and used as seasonings in

ARTICHOKE
Also known as globe artichoke. The large flower bud of a type of thistle, grown primarily in the Mediterranean and in California. The tightly packed cluster of tough, pointed, prickly leaves conceals tender, gray-green flesh at the vegetable's center—the heart.

A globe artichoke is easily prepared for cooking. While trimming, dip artichoke repeatedly in a mixture of water and lemon juice to prevent discoloring.

1. Cut or snap off the artichoke's stem at the base.

2. Cut off approximately 1 inch (2.5 cm) from the top of the artichoke.

3. Starting at the base, break off the toughest outer leaves, snapping them downward.

For an artichoke heart, continue snapping off leaves until only a cone of them remains. Cut these off to reveal the prickly choke; scrape it out. Pare off the remaining tough green outer skin.

cooking; most common are fruit-based chutneys, particularly mango. Available in ethnic markets, specialty-food stores and supermarket Asian-food sections.

CINNAMON
Popular sweet spice for flavoring both sweet and savory recipes. The aromatic bark of a type of evergreen tree, it is sold as whole dried strips—cinnamon sticks—or ground.

CORNMEAL
Granular flour, ground from the dried kernels of yellow or white corn, with a sweet, robust flavor. Sometimes known by the Italian term *polenta*. Most commercial cornmeal sold in food stores lacks the kernel's husk and germ and is available in fine or coarser grinds. Stone-ground cornmeal, made from whole corn kernels, produces a richer flour.

CREAM, HEAVY
Heavy whipping cream with a butterfat content of at least 36 percent. For the best flavor and cooking properties, purchase fresh cream, avoiding long-lasting varieties that have been processed by ultraheat methods. In Britain, use double cream.

EGGPLANT
Fruit vegetable, also known as aubergine, with tender, mildly earthy, sweet flesh. The shiny skins of eggplants vary in color

from purple to red and from yellow to white, and their shapes range from small and oval to long and slender to large and pear

shaped. The most common variety is large, purple and globular; but slender, purple Asian eggplants—smaller, more tender and with fewer seeds—are available with increasing frequency in food stores and vegetable markets.

FENNEL BULB
Crisp, refreshing, mildly anise–flavored bulb vegetable (below), sometimes called by its Italian name, *finocchio*. Another related variety of the bulb is valued for its fine, feathery leaves and stems, which are used as a fresh or dried herb, and for its small, crescent-shaped seeds, dried and used as a spice.

GINGER
The rhizome of the tropical ginger plant, which yields a sweet, strong-flavored spice. Whole ginger rhizomes, commonly but mistakenly called roots, may be purchased fresh in a food market or vegetable market. Ground, dried ginger is easily found in jars or tins in the supermarket spice section.

GRATIN
From the French word for "crust," term used to describe any oven-baked dish—usually cooked in a shallow, oval gratin dish—on which a golden brown crust of **bread crumbs,** cheese or creamy sauce is formed.

GRUYÈRE
Variety of Swiss cheese with a firm, smooth texture, small holes and a strong, tangy flavor.

HALF-AND-HALF
A commercial dairy product consisting of half milk and half light cream.

HAM HOCK
The narrow ankle section cut from a ham, often used in vegetable dishes to lend a smoky flavor.

JERUSALEM ARTICHOKE
Tuberous vegetable (below), native to North America, resembling small, lumpy potatoes. Although its subtle flavor is reminiscent of the **artichoke,** the two vegetables are not related. Its name is believed to derive from the Italian *girasole,* "sunflower," a plant to which it is related. Also called sunchoke.

KOHLRABI
Bulb-shaped vegetable related to cabbage, with thin, pale green skin, crisp white flesh and a delicate flavor resembling turnip.

MARJORAM
Pungent, aromatic herb used dried or fresh to season meats (particularly lamb), poultry, seafood, vegetables and eggs.

MUSTARD, DIJON
Dijon mustard is made in Dijon, France, from dark brown mustard seeds (unless otherwise marked *blanc*) and white wine or wine vinegar. Pale, fairly hot and sharp tasting, true Dijon mustard and non-French blends labeled "Dijon-style" are widely available in food stores.

LEEK
Sweet, moderately flavored member of the **onion** family, long and cylindrical in shape with a pale white root end and dark green leaves. Select firm, unblemished leeks, small to medium in size. Grown in sandy soil, the leafy-topped, multi-layered vegetables require thorough cleaning:

Trim off the tough ends of the dark green leaves. Trim off the roots. If a recipe calls for leek whites only, trim off the dark green leaves where they meet the slender pale green part of the stem. Slit the leek lengthwise three-fourths of the way down to the root end.

Vigorously swish the leek in a basin or sink filled with cold water. Drain and rinse again; check to make sure that no dirt remains between the tightly packed pale portion of the leaves.

NUTMEG

Popular baking spice that is the hard pit of the fruit of the nutmeg tree. May be bought already ground or, for fresher flavor, whole.

Whole nutmegs may be kept inside special nutmeg graters, which include hinged flaps that conceal a storage compartment.

Freshly grate nutmeg as needed, steadying one end of grater on work surface. Return unused portion of whole nutmeg to compartment.

OIL, OLIVE

Extra-virgin olive oil, extracted from olives on the first pressing without use of heat or chemicals, is valued for its distinctive fruity flavor. Many brands, varying in color and strength of flavor, are now available; choose one that suits your taste. The higher-priced extra-virgin olive oils usually are of better quality. Store in an airtight container away from heat and light.

OIL, SAFFLOWER

Pale, relatively flavorless oil used in dressings and for cooking.

OIL, SESAME

Rich, flavorful and aromatic oil pressed from sesame seeds. Those from China and Japan are usually made with roasted sesame seeds, resulting in a darker, stronger oil used as a flavoring ingredient; its low burning temperature and intense flavor make it unsuitable for using alone for cooking. Middle Eastern and Western forms of the oil, made from raw seeds, are lighter in color and taste, and may be used for cooking.

OKRA

Small, mild, slender green vegetable pods, about 1½–3 inches (4–7.5 cm) in length, with crisp outer flesh and thick, mucilaginous juices when cooked.

ONION, GREEN

Variety of onion harvested immature, leaves and all, before its bulb has formed. Green and white parts may both be enjoyed, raw or cooked, for their mild but still pronounced onion flavor. Also called spring onion or scallion.

ONION, RED

Mild, sweet variety of onion with purplish red skin and red-tinged white flesh. Also known as Spanish onion.

ONION, WHITE BOILING

Small, pungent onion, usually about 1 inch (2.5 cm) in diameter.

ONION, YELLOW

Common, white-fleshed, strong-flavored onion distinguished by its dry, yellowish brown skin.

OREGANO

Aromatic, pungent and spicy Mediterranean herb—also known as wild marjoram—used fresh or dried as a seasoning for all kinds of savory dishes. Especially popular with **tomatoes** and other vegetables.

PAPRIKA

Powdered spice derived from the dried paprika pepper; popular in several European cuisines and available in sweet, mild and hot forms. Hungarian paprika is the best, but Spanish paprika, which is mild, may also be used. Buy in small quantities from shops with a high turnover, to ensure a fresh, flavorful supply.

PARMESAN CHEESE

Hard, thick-crusted Italian cow's milk cheese with a sharp, salty, full flavor resulting from at least two years of aging. Buy in block form, to grate fresh as needed. The finest Italian variety is designated parmigiano-reggiano.

PARSLEY

This widely used fresh herb is available in two varieties: the more popular curly-leaf type and a flat-leaf type, also known as Italian parsley (shown below).

PARSNIP

Root vegetable similar in shape and texture to the carrot, but with ivory flesh and an appealingly sweet flavor.

PEPPER

Pepper, the most common of all savory spices, is best purchased as whole peppercorns, to be ground in a pepper mill as needed, or coarsely crushed. Pungent black peppercorns derive from slightly underripe pepper berries, whose hulls oxidize as they dry. Milder white peppercorns come from fully ripened berries, with the husks removed before drying.

PINE NUTS

Small, ivory seeds extracted from the cones of a species of pine tree, with a rich, slightly resinous flavor. Used whole as an ingredient or garnish, or puréed as a thickener. Also known by the Italian *pinoli*.

PROSCIUTTO

Italian raw ham, a specialty of Parma, cured by dry-salting for one month, followed by air-drying in cool curing rooms for half a year or longer. Usually cut into tissue-thin slices, the better to appreciate its intense flavor and deep pink color.

RED CURRANT JELLY

Tart, bright red preserve made from fresh red currants, enjoyed simply spread on bread or muffins, or used as an ingredient to add bright color and sharp, sweet flavor to other dishes.

RED PEPPER FLAKES

Coarsely ground flakes of dried red chilies, including seeds, which add moderately hot flavor to the foods they season.

RICE, ARBORIO
Popular Italian variety of rice with short, round grains high in starch content, which creates a creamy, saucelike consistency during cooking. Available in Italian delicatessens and well-stocked food stores.

ROSEMARY
Mediterranean herb, used either fresh or dried, with a strong aromatic flavor well suited to lamb and veal, as well as poultry and vegetables. Strong in flavor, it should be used sparingly, except when grilling.

RUTABAGA
Root vegetable resembling a large turnip, with sweet, pale yellow-orange flesh. Also known as swede or Swedish turnip.

SAGE
Pungent herb, used either fresh or dried, that goes particularly well with fresh or cured pork, lamb, veal, poultry or vegetables.

SHALLOT
Small member of the **onion** family with brown skin, white-to-purple flesh and a flavor resembling a cross between sweet onion and garlic.

SOY SAUCE
Asian seasoning and condiment usually made from soybeans, wheat or other grain, salt and water. Seek out good-quality imported soy sauces; Chinese brands tend to be markedly saltier than Japanese.

SPINACH
Choose smaller, more tender spinach leaves if possible. Be sure to wash thoroughly to eliminate all dirt and sand: Put the spinach leaves in a sink or large basin and fill with cold water to cover them thoroughly. Agitate the leaves in the water to remove their dirt. Then lift the leaves out of the water and set aside. Drain the sink or basin thoroughly and rinse out all dirt and sand. Repeat the procedure until no grit remains.

SUGAR, BROWN
A rich-tasting, fine-textured granulated sugar combined with molasses in varying quantities to yield light or dark varieties.

TARRAGON
Fragrant, distinctively sweet herb used fresh or dried as a seasoning for vegetables, salads, chicken, light meats, seafood and eggs.

THYME
Fragrant, clean-tasting, small-leaved herb popular fresh or dried as a seasoning for poultry, light meats, seafood or vegetables.

TOMATOES
During summer, when tomatoes are in season, use the best sun-ripened tomatoes you can find. At other times of year, plum tomatoes, sometimes called Roma or egg tomatoes, are likely to have the best flavor and texture.

VERMOUTH
Dry or sweet wine commercially enhanced with herbs and barks.

VINAIGRETTE
Literally "little vinegar," a classic French dressing or sauce for salad greens, vegetables, meats, poultry or seafood. A combination of **vinegar** or some other acid such as lemon juice, seasonings and oil.

SQUASHES
Native to the Americas, squashes are divided into two main types: thin-skinned summer squashes, such as zucchini (courgettes) and pattypan, and hard, tough-skinned winter squashes, such as acorn, butternut and pumpkin. The tender flesh of summer squashes cooks more quickly than the firm, usually sweet flesh of winter varieties.

Acorn Squash

Pattypan Squash

Preparing Winter Squash for Cooking
Use a heavy, sharp kitchen knife to cut open the squash; if its skin is very hard, use a kitchen mallet to tap the knife carefully once it is securely wedged in the squash.

Using a sharp-edged spoon, scrape out all seeds and fibers.

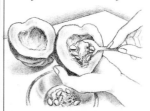

VINEGAR
Literally "sour" wine, vinegar results when certain strains of yeast cause wine—or some other alcoholic liquid such as apple cider or rice wine—to ferment for a second time, turning it acidic. The best-quality wine vinegars begin with good-quality wine. Red wine vinegar, like the wine from which it is made, has a more robust flavor than vinegar produced from white wine. Balsamic vinegar, a specialty of Modena, Italy, is a vinegar made from reduced grape juice and aged for many years. Flavored vinegars are made by adding herbs such as tarragon and dill or fruits such as raspberries.

WATER CHESTNUTS
Walnut-sized bulbs of an Asian plant grown in water, with brown skins concealing a refreshingly crisp, slightly sweet white flesh. Most often sold in cans already peeled and sometimes sliced or chopped, water chestnuts are sometimes found fresh in Asian food stores.

ZEST
Thin, brightly colored, outermost layer of a citrus fruit's peel, containing most of its aromatic essential oils—a lively source of flavor. Zest may be removed with a simple tool known as a zester, drawn across the fruit's skin to cut off the zest in thin strips; with a fine hand-held grater; or in wide strips with a vegetable peeler or a paring knife held almost parallel to the fruit's skin. Zest removed with the latter two tools may then be thinly sliced or chopped on a cutting board.

Index

Acknowledgments

The publishers would like to thank the following people and organizations for their generous assistance and support in producing this book:
Sharon C. Lott, Stephen W. Griswold, James Obata, Tara Brown, Ken DellaPenta, the buyers for Gardener's Eden, and the buyers
and store managers for Pottery Barn and Williams-Sonoma stores.

The following kindly lent props for the photography:
Biordi Art Imports, Fillamento, Stephanie Greenleigh, Wendely Harvey, Sue Fisher King, Karen Nicks,
Lorraine and Judson Puckett, Sue White and Chuck Williams.